Armlocks

To Chris,
Best Wishes
Neil Adams

ARMLOCKS
JUDO MASTERCLASS TECHNIQUES
NEIL ADAMS

IPPON/CROWOOD

First published in 1989 by
The Crowood Press
Ramsbury, Marlborough,
Wiltshire SN8 2HE

© Nicolas Soames 1989

All rights reserved. No part of this publication may be reproduced or transmitted in any form or by any means, electronic or mechanical, including photocopy, recording, or any information storage and retrieval system without permission in writing from the publishers.

British Library Cataloguing in Publication Data

Adams, Neil *1958–*
  Armlocks.
  1. Judo –Manuals
  I. Title II. Soames, Nicolas, *1950–*
  796.8'152

ISBN 1-85223-247-1

Acknowledgements

Special thanks are due to David Finch for his painstaking camera work and helpful advice on details of presentation. Thanks also to Benjamin Soames who stepped in as uke at the last minute after a particularly gruelling judo session.

Finally, I would like to express my gratitude to the Budokwai in London. My club throughout my senior contest career, they supported me handsomely, and generously made the small dojo available for the photo sessions.

Typeset by Avonset, Midsomer Norton, Bath
Printed in Great Britain by Dotesios Printers Ltd., Trowbridge, Wiltshire

Contents

Foreword	6
Armlocks: a Personal View	7
A History of Armlocks	8
Juji-gatame	14
Finishing Juji-gatame	38
Ude-gatame	44
Ude-garami	49
Waki-gatame	57
Standing Armlocks	59
Hara-gatame	65
Special Combinations	68
Self-defence	76
Competition Armlocks	80
Afterword	94
Index	96

Foreword

Armlocks have always been accorded a prominent role in judo, not least because of their immediate effectiveness. Practised in most ju-jitsu schools, they came under the general terminology of *kansetsu-waza,* or joint locks. The third section of the groundwork kata, *katame-no-kata,* was devoted to armlocks, with the main five demonstrated: *ude-garami, juji-gatame, ude-gatame, hiza-gatame* and *ashi-garami.*

When Yukio Tani brought judo to widespread notice in Britain in the first decade of the twentieth century by touring the music-halls to take on all comers, the armlock was much in evidence. One of his special techniques was a flying armlock which had powerful boxers and wrestlers submitting anxiously. That Tani's exploits made a noted impression on his British audience is borne out by Bernard Shaw's reference to him in his play, *Major Barbara:* the character Todger Fairmile confesses to having submitted to the 'Jap wrestler' but only when his arms were going to break!

But as the competition side of judo developed over the following decades, it was the West that took the lead with armlocks. In men's judo in the United Kingdom today as many as sixty per cent of contests won on the gound are armlock victories, while the percentage in Japan is much smaller – often less than twenty-five per cent.

Ever since winning the 1981 World Championships with juji-gatame, Neil Adams has been regarded as one of the finest exponents of armlocks and there could have been no more appropriate author for a specialist book on the subject. It came as no surprise that, when invited to teach a technique at the Kodokan in Tokyo, he was specifically asked to demonstrate juji-gatame.

But in addition to the variety of turns into juji-gatame which he demonstrated throughout his extensive contest career, he has also made a specialist study of other armlocks – and their use in *tachiwaza* as well as *newaza.*

Here, for the first time, he concentrates on armlocks alone, including most of the techniques that are seen on the modern contest mat. It is an absorbing and fascinating study which will doubtless be regarded as the handbook of the subject for decades to come.

Nicolas Soames
Masterclass Series Editor

Armlocks: a Personal View

The armlock has been one of the most successful groundwork skills of the 1980s and has developed to such a degree that judoka from all over the world are specialising in the complexities of the technique.

I was first made aware of *juji-gatame*, the most popular of the contest armlocks, at the 1976 Junior World Championships, when I saw Yastkevich of the Soviet Union win the title by turning a Japanese player from his knees on to his back with a brilliantly applied specialist movement, concluded by a swiftly applied juji-gatame. Until that time I had not been particularly interested in *newaza*, but after witnessing this well-rehearsed move I decided to see if I could work and improve on it and perhaps add it to my judo repertoire.

At this stage in my judo career I had never used a video to study technique but kept a carefully documented record of all the new ideas which impressed me. I returned to my London club with my notes, eager to explore the possibilities of this new armlock with my training partner.

I must have either written down Yastkevich's technique incorrectly or misunderstood it because my armlock was technically very different although it did eventually win me my world title in the final of the 1981 World Championships in Holland. My interpretation of Yastkevich's armlock may have been very successful but the inaccuracy of my notes taught me some invaluable lessons. The first was the importance of using a video, and the second, the possibility of applying the turn into juji-gatame in different ways, and, as I was later to discover, from many different positions.

I found it very difficult to catch my opponents with the turn at first and I realised that I would have to do a substantial amount of repetition work to become proficient with it.

I began practising the turn against lower grades, working my way up to the Dan grades as I got better until the time came to unleash the technique in competition.

In the early days I could only attack my opponent if he was on his hands and knees and in a defensive newaza position. This restricted my new move and forced me to look at some different possibilities to help me in the original situations of contest. I started to create turns into juji-gatame off my back and found that as long as I had control of the arm and head I was able to do many variations. These are explained in detail in Chapter 3.

The only other type of armlock that I have ever used is a standing armlock. It has been quite successful since the early 1970s and although it has never really scored many ippons it has been particularly useful in breaking grips, especially important as gripping has now become such an intrinsic part of modern-day judo.

I will continue to look for new ways of applying armlocks and I would like to think that I have contributed in some way towards developing a few of the more modern methods.

Technically, judo has progressed more quickly than anyone could have imagined since it became an Olympic sport in 1964 and I am sure it will continue to exceed my expectations. I will watch its progress with interest.

A History of Armlocks

It is almost impossible to trace the exact origins of the armlock although different forms have been used throughout the ages by various fighting traditions. Interestingly there is little if any evidence for the development of the armlock in the West. The hammerlock (where the arm is trapped up an opponent's back) seems to have a Western trademark and probably came from a form of wrestling, although there are no armlocks allowed in 'free-style' or 'Graeco–Roman' style wrestling.

So where did the armlock originate and how has it developed over the years?

It seems that the Eastern fighting arts have been the main force behind the development of armlocks, with ju-jitsu, aikido, judo and various Chinese systems being the most prominent. However, it is the Soviet form of wrestling called *sambo*, a relatively modern form of combat, that has been the main contributor to the armlocks of today.

We are unsure as to the exact origins of ju-jitsu. Many think that it was brought over from China in the 1660s although this story never completely convinced Jigoro Kano, who clarified his own analysis of ju-jitsu at the turn of the century to form modern-day judo.

Ju-jitsu was originally formed as a method of defence and offence without weapons and it was practised in the East as a military art, together with types of fencing and archery. In Japan there were many forms of ju-jitsu and competitions between the opposing schools often occurred; however, it was not until Kano's interpretation that one style stood out above the rest.

In the early days techniques were developed to lock almost all parts of the body, some of which could be very dangerous. There were locks to wrists, spine, elbows, legs and fingers, and many of these have been incorporated into contemporary martial arts. Aikido for example combines wristlocks, armlocks and fingerlocks with throwing techniques. It is particularly well known for the control with which these are practised and applied.

Karate is now at the same stage as ju-jitsu was at the turn of the century, with its numerous styles all striving for supreme recognition. Although no locks are permitted in any of the styles, there are techniques consisting of blows to the leg joints which can be extremely dangerous and have to be practised with considerable control.

Surprisingly, Russian sambo wrestling (*sambo* in Russian means self-defence) is probably the closest relative to ju-jitsu, allowing armlocks, leglocks and all forms of throwing and ground moves. This form of wrestling was developed in the 1930s. However, it was only recently, during the 1960s, that the Russians revolutionised modern-day judo with their unorthodox techniques derived from sambo wrestling, thus opening up a whole new range of ideas for the modern judoka.

Judo was Dr Kano's form of ju-jitsu, which he developed with a safety structure in order that it could be practised without danger to life and limb. This enabled it to be introduced as part of the Japanese school curriculum, and although there were still ju-jitsu schools all over Japan, the initiative had passed to Kano's safer form of fighting.

In the 1950s people were beginning to look at judo in a different way, not just as a martial art but also as a sport. The first world cham-

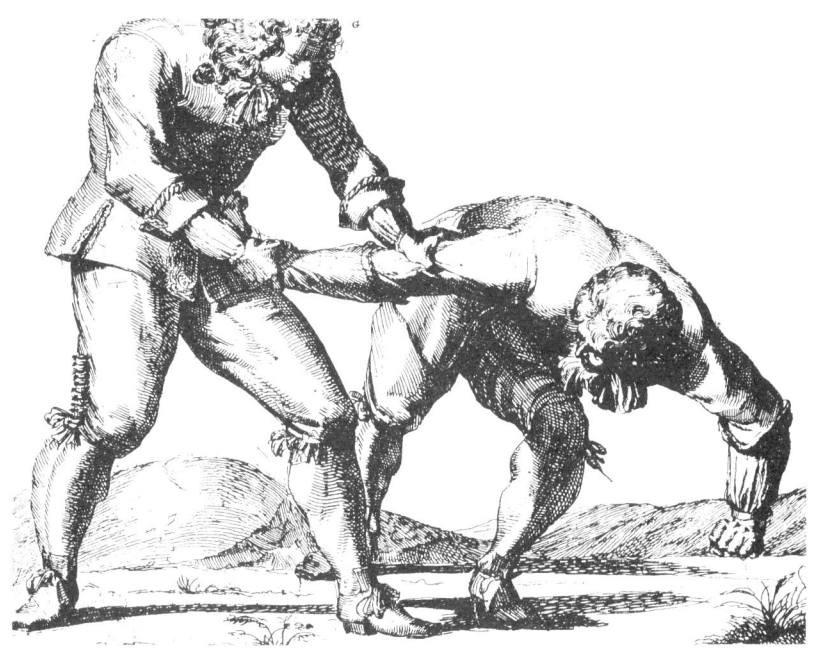

Fig 1 These two standing armlocks come from a collection of self-defence moves presented in a series of engravings by the seventeenth-century Dutch engraver, Romeyn de Hooghe, and based on the instructions of an early Dutch traveller to Japan.

pionships were in 1956 in Japan and each of the weight divisions was won by the Japanese. However, five years later a giant Dutchman called Anton Geesink beat the reigning World Champion Sone with a hold-down that left the Japanese judo followers in shock. The rest of the world realised that the Japanese could be beaten, and so commenced the emergence of the Europeans as a force in judo.

The possibility of judo being included in the 1964 Olympic games saw the rapid growth of the Soviet Union as a judo nation, and in 1962 they entered a team in the European Championships for the very first time. It was at these championships that everyone saw the similarities between sambo and judo, but no-one was prepared for the effect that the Soviets were going to have on the evolution of judo over the next twenty-five years. To say that they were unorthodox is an understatement, and it was particularly their numerous variations on

A HISTORY OF ARMLOCKS

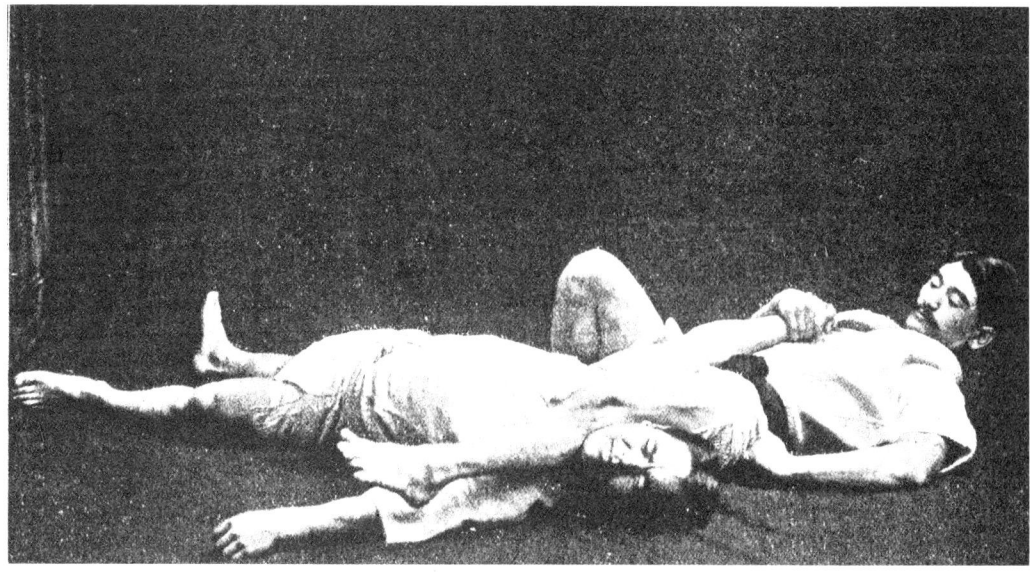

Fig 2 Things Japanese had a considerable vogue in Europe at the turn of the century. These photographs are amongst the illustrations to The Text-Book of Ju-Jitsu by S.K. Uyenishi, published in 1905.

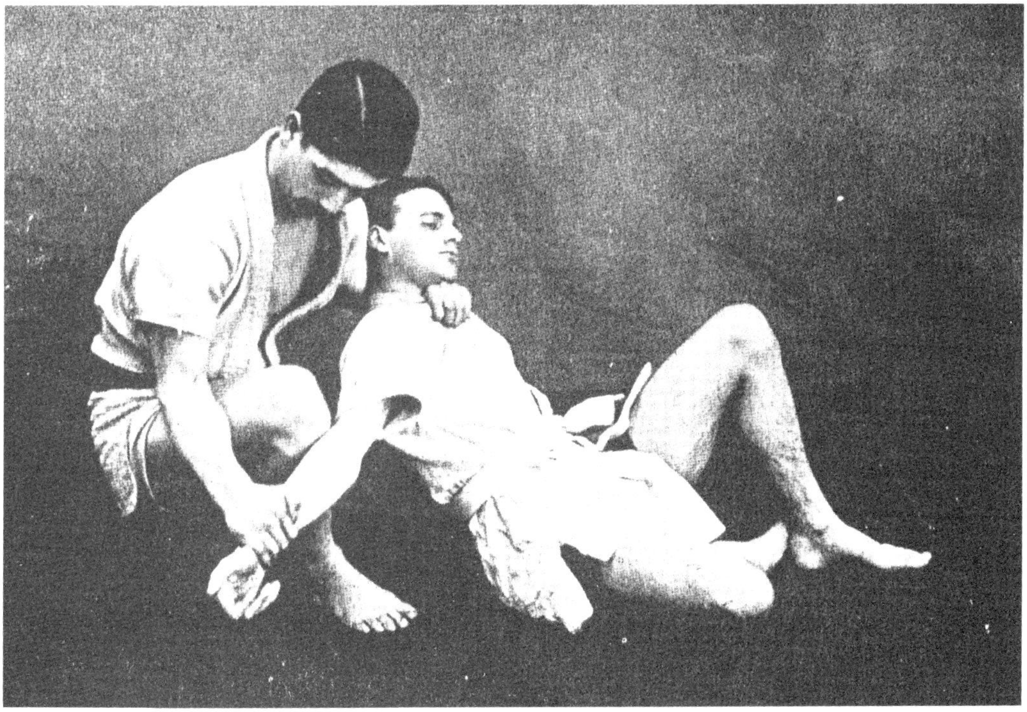

A HISTORY OF ARMLOCKS

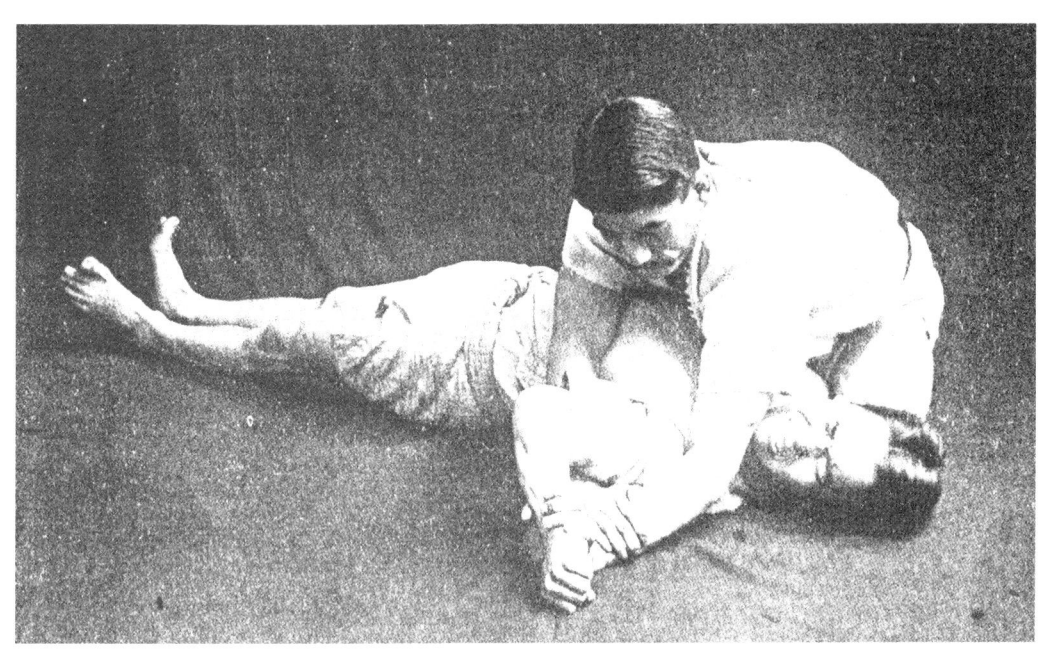

A HISTORY OF ARMLOCKS

Fig 3 In a spirited account of The Fine Art of Ju-jitsu, *published in 1906, Mrs Watts opened up the possibilities of practising the martial arts to women as well as men. Here she demonstrates two standing armlocks.*

armlocks which took everyone by surprise. Up until this time a flying juji-gatame had never been seen in competition, but it was apparent that these were very well-rehearsed moves from a very highly-trained team. The Soviets had a dramatic effect on their first European Championships and took home five medals.

Judo was indeed included in the 1964 Olympic games in Tokyo, and although it was omitted from the 1968 Mexico Olympics it was reinstated as a fully recognised Olympic sport in the 1972 Munich games.

This really saw the start of the development of judo world-wide, and it became apparent that just being Japanese did not guarantee judo success, because by now more sophisticated training methods were being used by different nations. Judoka from all over the world were beginning to train full-time, even if that meant travelling all over the world in order to get the necessary intensity and depth of training.

Major World, Olympic and European medals were now being spread amongst the nations of the world and judoka were perfecting more and more specialist moves. In fact it was another Soviet, Nevzerov, who in the Montreal Olympic games convincingly won the light-middleweight title, stamping his authority with his brilliant *tachiwaza* and his neatly applied juji-gatame in newaza. It seemed that juji-gatame was becoming a fashionable *tokui-waza,* and its development over the next decade was quite remarkable. The success that many of the Europeans were enjoying with the technique seemed to pose a threat to the Japanese. Although superbly accomplished, and still as a nation superior in depth, many were being beaten with a number of different armlocks, especially juji-gatame. It is strange that even to this day the Japanese have not changed their style of judo and endeavoured to fill probably the only chink in their armour.

Who knows where judo will go in the next twenty years, and what developments we will see. I personally would like to see a more traditional style of judo as I feel that our sport is becoming too heavily influenced by wrestling techniques. Having benefited from other fighting arts, for example by gaining the armlock as one of our specialist skills, we should continue to practise with an open mind. However, it is vital that in so doing we do not forget the form and spirit in which judo originated.

Juji-gatame

Juji-gatame is the most popular of all the armlocks, and is used by many of the top judoka in competitions. It can be applied in a variety of different forms, and from a wide range of situations.

To ensure that the technique gets 'ingrained', it is vital to practise *uchi-komi* (repetition) sufficiently. This is the case with all the techniques in this book. A good training partner is essential, with both judoka experimenting with the techniques in order to create new variations.

Note Any references to left or right in the following chapters are determined by the photographs in question. All of the techniques demonstrated can of course be performed on both sides, and must be practised as such.

Armlocks and safety

In judo you are expected to take exhaustion and even pain with equanimity. You are expected to struggle determinedly when caught in a hold, and even resist strangles with courage, though it is obviously common sense to submit before the limits of consciousness have been reached.

However, there is generally no point in continuing to resist against an armlock once the technique has taken effect. Long-term damage can occur to elbow joints if you have decided to play the hero and there are very few circumstances, even in a contest, where it is worth trying to hang on when an armlock is being applied. Just submit, so that you can use your arm another day.

There is also a responsibility within the tradition of judo, certainly in practice and generally in competition, for the person applying the armlock to ensure that he or she does not snap on a lock with a sharp and vicious movement, giving the opponent insufficient time to submit. Skill and style are important in judo, but so is care – and nowhere more so than in the use of armlocks.

Basic juji-gatame *(Fig 4(a))*

This is Kano's classic interpretation of juji-gatame. Notice that in (a) tori's left leg is lying across uke's head while his right leg is in a bent position. He is also wedging his right foot underneath uke's body, which prevents uke rolling towards tori. The leg controlling the head also prevents uke rolling away from tori.

Fig 4(a) Basic juji-gatame

Juji-gatame – modern style *(Fig 4(b))*

This is the juji-gatame that is almost always seen in judo now. Both of tori's legs are across uke's body and often, as in Fig 4(b) the feet are locked together to give extra security. This gives tori much better control of his opponent, particularly if he is resisting strongly.

Juji-gatame actually means 'cross hold' because the shape of the two bodies form a cross, and tori should be capable of holding uke in this position. This is relatively easy, of course, with the arm straight – uke risks injury to his elbow if he moves. But even if tori has not straightened the arm, he should be able to hold uke in this 'juji' position just with one arm lightly holding the bent elbow, and his legs firmly controlling uke's upper body. This is the first basic requirement of the famous juji-gatame.

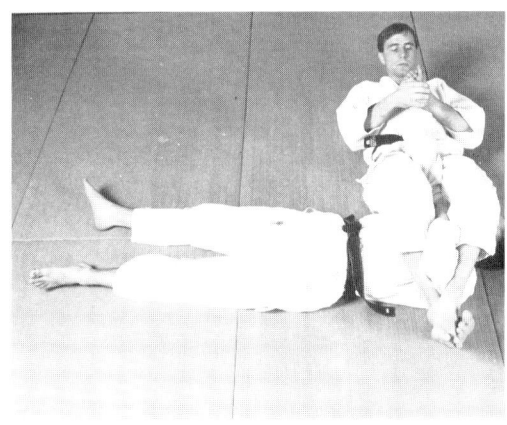

Fig 4(b)

JUJI-GATAME

Fig 5 Pillow juji-gatame.

Pillow juji-gatame *(Fig 5)*

I have called this variation 'pillow juji-gatame' because tori's left leg is underneath uke's head (like a pillow) while the right leg secures uke's left arm and head. By crossing his feet tori secures upper body control. To apply the armlock, tori, whose hips are turned towards uke's head, must fully extend the right arm from the shoulder ensuring that uke's thumb is pointed towards the ceiling in order to make the arm lock when tori pushes his hips forward.

Notice that tori has pulled uke's left arm towards him in order to gain maximum control of both arms.

Tip
Complete control of the head and arms is essential here because the angle at which the armlock is applied is unorthodox.

Sangaku-juji-gatame *(Fig 6)*

Sangaku translated means 'triangular' and refers to the shape of the legs around the arm and head. The technique is similar to the pillow juji-gatame with tori's left leg resting underneath uke's head. However, instead of trapping uke's left arm and shoulder, tori's right leg wraps directly around uke's neck. To secure the lock, tori places his right foot behind his left knee and lifts his hips upwards.

If you find it difficult to put your right foot behind the knee a slight adjustment with the hips is necessary. First turn your hips towards uke's head – this should enable you to make sufficient contact. Now turn your hips back square and you should find that a strangle and the armlock are applied simultaneously.

Fig 6 Sangaku-juji-gatame.

JUJI-GATAME

Kesa-gatame into juji-gatame (Fig 7)

Kesa-gatame (scarf hold) is so called because the right arm of tori passes around uke's neck like a scarf in order to control the head. It is one of the first hold-downs that judoka are taught and leads well into Kano's classical juji-gatame.

This move can be useful if you are trying to hold down a particularly strong opponent and you think that it will be a difficult task to secure the hold for the full thirty seconds. It is then necessary to change your tactics and move to an alternative situation as smoothly as possible. Because head and arm control are maintained all the time, it can make a nice combination technique.

(a) Tori has control of uke's right arm. This is placed under tori's armpit and across his chest. Tori spreads his legs to stabilise the technique.

(b) Tori steps across uke's body, placing his foot at the opposite side of his head and at the same time bringing his right leg to the right side of uke – ensuring that at all times he has control of his arm.

(c) Tori then lies on his back and traps uke's head with his left leg, simultaneously wedging his right foot underneath uke's body. The hand and arm positions of tori remain steady and the armlock is applied by lifting the hips.

Flying juji-gatame *(Fig 8)*

(Divisenko)

This particular variation of the flying juji-gatame was performed by Divisenko of the Soviet Union in the European Championships in the under 95 kilo category against Neureuther of West Germany. A great spirit of commitment is essential for this attack. It is this type of unorthodox technique that has revolutionised modern-day judo.

Note It is interesting to note that if you look at the clock in this series of photographs, it took less than three seconds from beginning to end for Divisenko to gain his submission.

(a) Here you can see the total commitment of Divisenko, leaping off the ground and leaving his bewildered opponent in a semi-crouched position.

(b) Divisenko's head has landed almost between Neureuther's feet at the same time as his right leg has been forced up into the left armpit thus ruining the German's balance.

(c) and (d) Throughout the technique Divisenko must maintain control of Neureuther's right arm and this can be done by holding the sleeve of the right arm with one or both hands, or by simply trapping the arm between the forearm and upper body as he leaps off the ground.

The importance of arm control can be seen here. Because of the momentum of the attack Neureuther has been thrown forwards off his feet, but insufficient control of the arm at this stage would probably have meant failure of the technique.

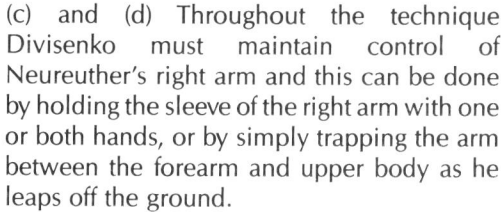 

 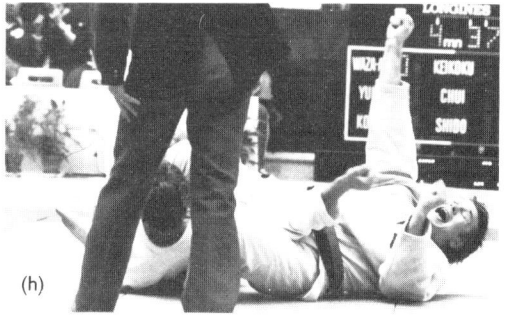

(e),(f),(g) and (h)   Divisenko applies so much pressure to the arm that the German is forced to somersault over on to his back and rapidly submit to save his arm from being broken.

JUJI-GATAME

Turns into juji-gatame

There are many different turns into juji-gatame, each finishing with the same basic armlock. The technicalities of the turns are very important and it must not be forgotten that control of the head is as important as control of the arm(s), and that mastery of these turns is very largely dependent on getting the position of the legs right.

Turn 1 *(Fig 9)*

(Left arm, left shoulder)

(a) Tori is demonstrating a very effective way of controlling uke's arm by catching uke's left wrist with the right hand and simultaneously passing the left hand underneath uke's arm and gripping his own right wrist. By pulling uke's arm inwards against his chest, tori can now commence the attack by keeping the arm and shoulder tight throughout the movement.

Tori's left foot is wedged underneath uke's left leg and at the same time tori sits on uke's back, thus preventing him from standing up to avoid the technique.

JUJI-GATAME

(b) Tori now rolls on to his left shoulder and prepares to take his right leg underneath uke's head. This can sometimes be quite difficult to do, but by pushing a wedged-shaped hand underneath uke's chin and forcing his head to turn, tori has now put himself in the ideal position to turn his opponent.

(c) Once the leg is wrapped around the head, tori resumes the original arm control ready for the turn.

(d) This shows how important the head control is and how the turning action must be continued while ensuring that pressure is applied to the arm.

(e) Once uke is on his back tori's leg control of the head and upper body is important. The arm is locked by lifting the hips and at the same time pulling and extending uke's arm from the shoulder joint.

JUJI-GATAME

Turn 2 *(Fig 10)*
(Yastkevich)

This particular variation is the one that influenced my own juji-gatame some years after first seeing it. It was in the final of the 1976 Junior World Championships that I saw Yastkevich turn his Japanese opponent on to his back with this turn.

(a) The turn begins in much the same way as the previous one, with the left foot placed in the same position and the right foot poised ready to pass underneath uke's head. However, the arm control is completely different with tori's right arm hooking uke's left arm. The normal reaction for uke from this position is to pull his arm in towards his body to defend against the lock. This actually helps tori as the arm is now well controlled and ready for the turn.

(b) Instead of tori rolling on to his left shoulder, he now rolls on to his right one (an easy way to remember is: right arm in, right shoulder roll) and prepares to take his right leg underneath uke's head. Uke's head has now been forced into the mat. This sometimes means that a wedged hand is needed to force the head upwards and around in order to get the right leg underneath uke's head.

JUJI-GATAME

(c) Before tori is able to continue with the turn it is essential that uke's head is facing downwards. Tori is now ready to use his free left hand to turn uke on to his back.

(d) Tori has taken uke's far (right) leg, but it is possible to take either right or left.

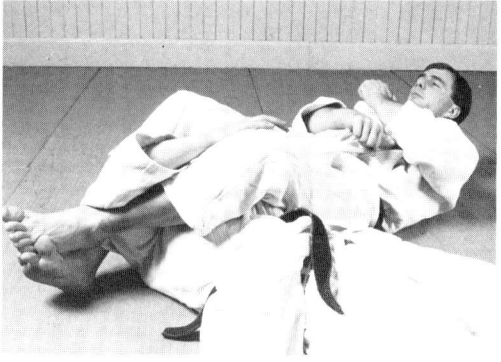

(e) Tori now pulls uke's leg around his own head in a circular movement and rotates uke on to his back.

(f) Taking uke's arm towards the head to break uke's grip, tori straightens his body and lifts his hips to apply the lock.

JUJI-GATAME

Turn 3 *(Fig 11)*

(Adams)

This variation was my own interpretation of Yastkevich's turn and developed into one of my most successful contest techniques. It is characterised by the lifting action between uke's legs.

(a) Here you can see me using my head in order to roll on to my right shoulder. This prevents me dropping on to my shoulder and possibly injuring myself.

(b) This is the start of a sequence that shows me turning Picken of Australia over in the 1980 Moscow Olympics. It uses the same hand and arm control as described in Turn 1.

We see that I have rolled on to my right shoulder and taken my left foot through the middle of my opponent's legs in order to start my lifting action while simultaneously applying pressure to his left arm.

JUJI-GATAME

(c) To relieve the pressure on his arm my opponent is forced to somersault on to his back.

(d) Although I have to temporarily let go of the arm with my right hand, my left arm is hooking and controlling his arm as I am turning my opponent over.

(e) Now it is important that I control my opponent's head and body with my legs. I do this by forcing my left leg into my opponent's midsection and at the same time forcing his head towards the mat with my right leg to prevent him from sitting forwards.

(f) I now proceed to straighten his arm in the normal manner – keeping the pressure on the arm at all times – taking it towards the head first, then straightening my hips to finish the move.

25

JUJI-GATAME

Turn 4 *(Fig 12)*

(Forward roll juji-gatame)

(a) Tori once again starts the technique by wedging his left foot behind his opponent's left leg and simultaneously gripping uke's belt with his left hand. He pulls the belt upwards and at the same time forces uke's left leg outwards so that he has enough space to put his head, thus starting the rolling action.

(b) Tori hooks the left arm and throws his head between uke's leg and arm, keeping hold of the belt throughout the move.

(c) Tori now reaches the crucial part of the turn and must trap his head as soon as possible to prevent uke from rolling on to his right leg.

(d) and (e) Tori has moved his right leg outwards so that he can wrap it around uke's head – nudged into place by tori's forearm – and finish the move in the normal manner.

Turn 5 *(Fig 13)*
(Pillow sangaku-juji-gatame)

(a) It is sometimes difficult to get the right leg underneath your opponent's head, especially if he has gripped your leg with his hand.

(b) If this occurs tori must push the head upwards with his right leg to start the turn. He passes his left hand through uke's left arm and controls it in the usual way. At the same time tori uses his left leg to push uke's right leg and his right leg to push uke's head so that he can begin to roll him on to his back.

(c) He then rotates uke on to his back.

(d) To stop uke sitting up, tori must turn his hips so that uke's head rests on tori's right leg, pillow-fashion. Tori now places his right foot behind his left knee and applies the juji-gatame sangaku-jime technique.

If you find it difficult to place your foot behind your knee you must rotate your hips towards uke's head and adjust the position of your body accordingly.

JUJI-GATAME

Turn 6 *(Fig 14)*

(Neil Eckersley – leg control)

Neil Eckersley's technique is very similar to Yastkevich's *(see* Turn 2). The interesting difference is that before he starts his rolling action, Neil secures a unique movement with his right foot.

While hooking his opponent's right arm with his own, tori pulls uke back towards himself, allowing enough space to slide his left foot underneath uke's body, and trapping uke's right knee with his left foot. Tori now turns his opponent in the same way as Yastkevich does, using his foot to pull the legs towards him, and keeping control of uke's left arm throughout the technique. Tori then proceeds to pull the right leg around his head (as in Turn 2).

Turn 7 *(Fig 15)*
(Arm-hook and leg spin)

(a) As before we start with tori's left foot wedged behind uke's left leg and tori hooking uke's left arm with his right arm.

(b) Tori now swings his right leg over uke's head and secures a grip on his belt with his left hand. He proceeds to turn uke by pulling downwards with the belt and at the same time sits down.

(c) Tori then overturns uke placing his left foot between uke's legs and using his secured left arm to lever uke on to his back.

(d) It is important to control uke's head as quickly as possible because he can sometimes turn very rapidly.

(e) The lock is then applied by tori lifting his hips and pulling on the straight arm.

JUJI-GATAME

Turn 8 *(Fig 16(a)–(f))*

(Seisenbacher)

Peter Seisenbacher the double Olympic champion has his own variation on juji-gatame. Although he uses a couple of the turn-overs previously explained, he doesn't always waste his energy on the turns and so finishes the armlock while his opponents are still lying face down. This requires considerable and constant pressure on the arm.

(a) Tori has hooked his opponent's left arm and has used his right arm to stabilise the movement.

(b) Tori now brings his right knee to the side of uke's head, placing his foot across the back of uke's neck.

(c) Tori uses his knee to push uke's head to the side. At the same time he pulls uke's arm in the opposite direction while forcing his own hips into the mat, thus applying the armlock.

Securing a loose head

At all times with juji-gatame it is essential that you have control of your opponent's head. On many occasions the roll has been lost when uke tries to stand up and succeeds in lifting his head.

(d) Here is a typical example of this happening, with uke pushing upwards with his right arm in order to try and stand up and therefore stop the turn.

(e) To prevent this tori uses his right leg to sweep the arm away and flatten uke out.

(f) Tori can now apply a Seisenbacher juji-gatame face down or turn uke on to his back with one of the other turns.

Fig 17 A reverse juji-gatame seen at the 1988 Tournoi de Paris. Note the perfect control, with the controlling hand on the elbow joint itself.

JUJI-GATAME

Spins into juji-gatame

In my early competition days I was always looking for different variations on juji-gatame. I began to think that an attack off my back would be unusual especially if I could develop a number of methods of turning my opponent over from this position. Many judoka find themselves lying on their backs during competition and it can be a great confidence booster if they are able to turn their opponents' attacks to their own advantage.

Spin 1 *(Fig 18)*

(Head control)

(a) Tori has uke in a kneeling position between his legs with uke gripping tori's left lapel with his right hand.

JUJI-GATAME

(b) and (c) It is important that tori uses his legs to control the attack from uke, so he now places his left forearm across uke's right arm and pivots his hips in a circular motion, at the same time bringing his left leg around uke's head.

(d) and (e) Tori now uses his leg to push uke's head downwards towards the mat and forces him on to his back to apply the lock.

JUJI-GATAME

Spin 2 *(Fig 19)*

(a) and (b) Tori has started with an attack along the lines of Spin 1.

(c) However, instead of turning away, uke has closed in on tori's attacking leg and forced tori's legs backwards towards the mat, making the first spin impossible.

(d) In this situation it is important for tori to continue the spinning action, pushing against uke's right leg in order to pull his head through the gap.

JUJI-GATAME

(e) and (f) Uke's head has now been forced down into the mat and tori, who is lying on his left shoulder, can proceed to pull uke's left leg around his head.

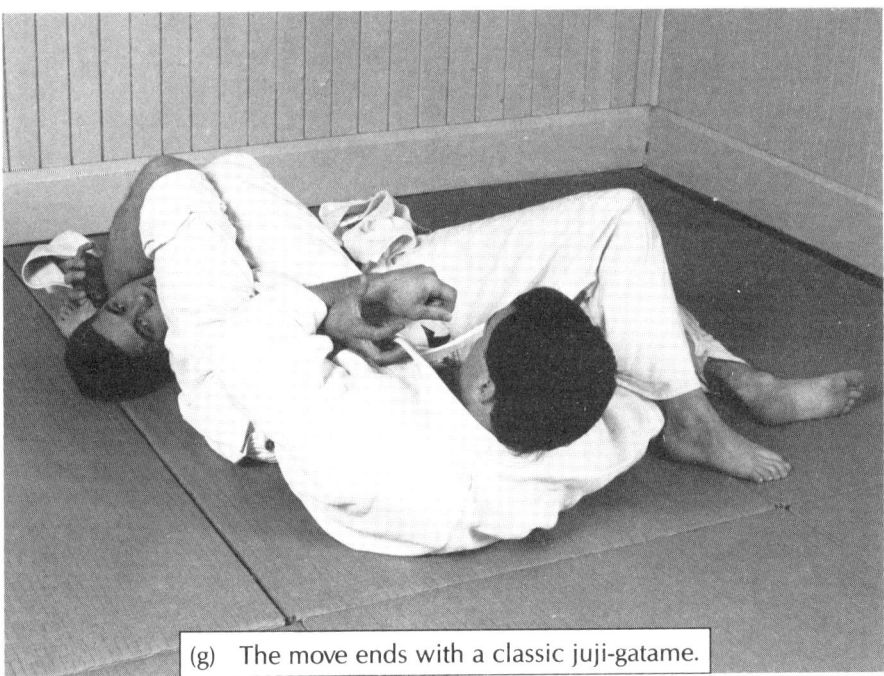

(g) The move ends with a classic juji-gatame.

Spin 3 *(Fig 20)*

Sangaku into juji-gatame

(a) Tori has pushed uke's head to the left whilst spinning to his right.

(b) This enables tori to place his right knee across the back of uke's neck.

(c) and (d) Placing his right foot behind his left knee tori applies the sangaku. He then forces uke on to his back and swiftly applies the armlock.

Spin 4 *(Fig 21)*

(a) Although the starting position for Spin 4 is the same as for the others the difference is that in order to start the technique a space must be created between uke and tori and the lock applied with uke lying face down.

(b) Tori has turned his hips and body to the right and placed his right foot against uke's left leg.

(c) Controlling uke's arm with his left arm tori then pushes uke's left leg away and brings uke's head down on to the mat, simultaneously taking his left leg around uke's head.

(d) Tori now pushes his hips downwards and at the same time pulls uke's arm across his hips to apply the lock.

Finishing Juji-gatame

Many judoka find it extremely difficult to straighten uke's arm and so finish the juji-gatame. However, there are some rules which make the technique easier. Most importantly, the mistake that many judoka make is to rush the technique, resulting in lack of control. Once uke is on his back the advantage is with tori, and he must make sure he has complete control of uke before attempting to straighten his arm.

Double Armlock 1 *(Fig 22)*

(Control with the legs)

The legs are the strongest part of the body and tori must use them throughout the technique. By crossing his feet and simultaneously pulling uke's right shoulder towards him with his legs he gains maximum control of uke. He now has a double opportunity for an armlock. Tori can either push uke's right arm upwards with his right hand, gripping the elbow between his knees to gain one armlock, or roll on to his back and apply a normal juji-gatame on uke's left arm.

Double Armlock 2 *(Fig 23)*

(Sangaku leg control)

(a) Tori attacks from the normal position with his left arm hooking uke's left arm.

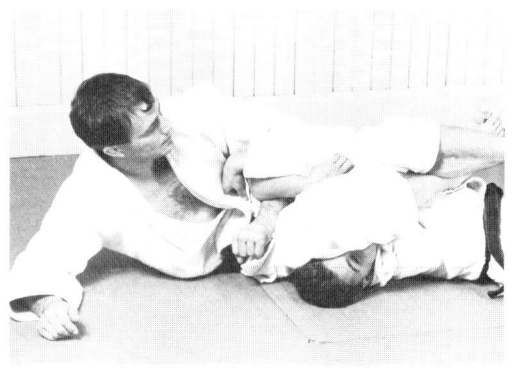

(b) He forces uke's right arm towards uke's head by falling on to his right side. Tori puts his right foot behind his own left knee.

(c) To complete the technique tori wedges his left foot under uke's left side and pulls his hips square to the mat. He pulls on uke's left arm to apply juji-gatame and can then lock uke's other arm by pushing his wrist upwards.

FINISHING JUJI-GATAME

Pressure lock with the leg *(Fig 24)*

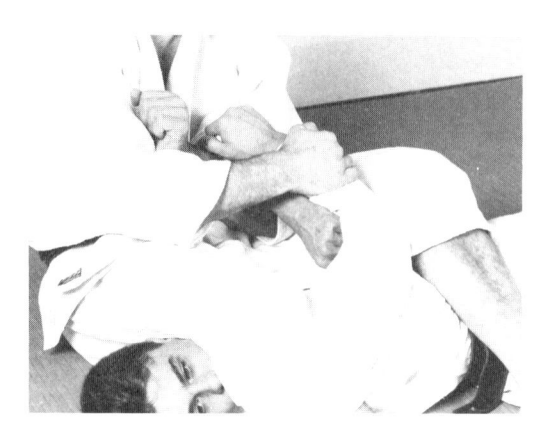

(a) When uke resists from this position he often grips his own opposite lapels, keeping his elbows raised in the air. Tori then pushes uke's arms flat against uke's body.

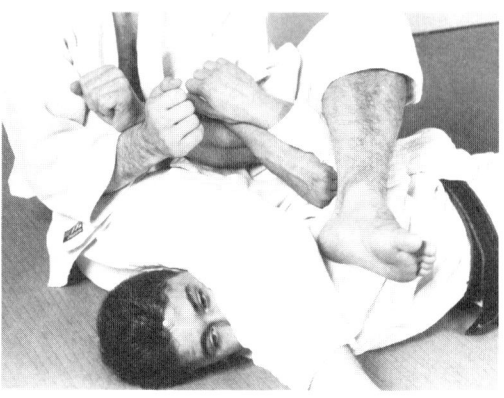

(b) Tori lifts his left leg and pushes it downwards over uke's right arm.

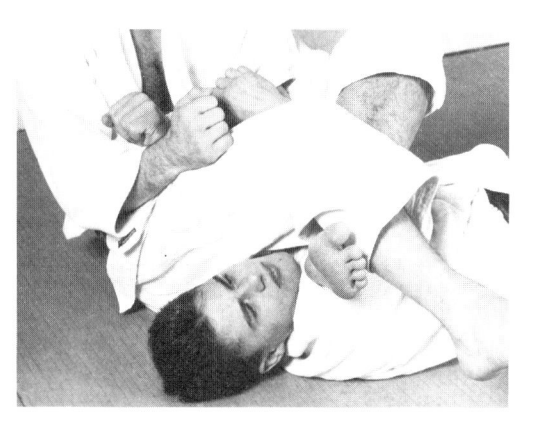

(c) Tori now lifts his right leg over uke's head and places his left foot behind his right knee. He pushes downwards with his legs and pulls against uke's arms. This has a spring effect on the arms and can be extremely painful and difficult for uke to resist.

FINISHING JUJI-GATAME

Levers

This is all about simple mechanical advantages that may be used to supplement the power of individual muscles.

Body levers *(Fig 25)*

Tori hooks uke's arms with his left arm and grips his own right lapel with his left hand. Tori falls on to his right side towards uke's head, thus using his body to lever uke's arm into a lock.

Note This is a technique I found useful in the 1981 World Championships.

Leg and hand levers *(Fig 26)*

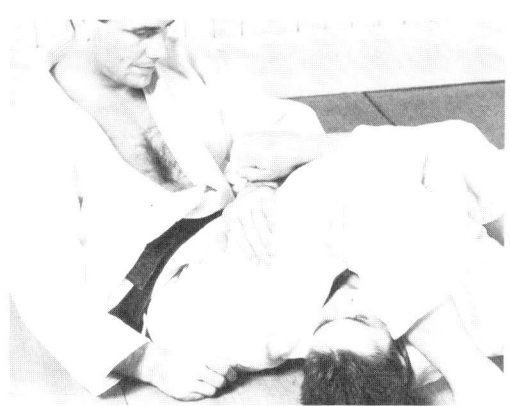

Tori's left arm hooks uke's arm. He places his left hand over his right thigh using his leg and hand to lever uke's arm in the direction of uke's head.

Hand position *(Fig 27)*

Tori applies pressure to uke's arm by leaning towards his head, and must look for any possible part of uke's arm to take so that he can finish the armlock. By taking the side of his right wrist under and against uke's left wrist, he attacks the weakest part of uke's arm.

It is not always necessary or possible to use a two-handed lever for an armlock. Identical results can be achieved using one arm.

FINISHING JUJI-GATAME

Double arm lever *(Fig 28)*

(a) Tori levers uke's arms towards his head using the hand lever method, and lies on his right side.

(b) Tori passes his right hand underneath uke's arms and places the side of his right wrist against uke's left wrist.

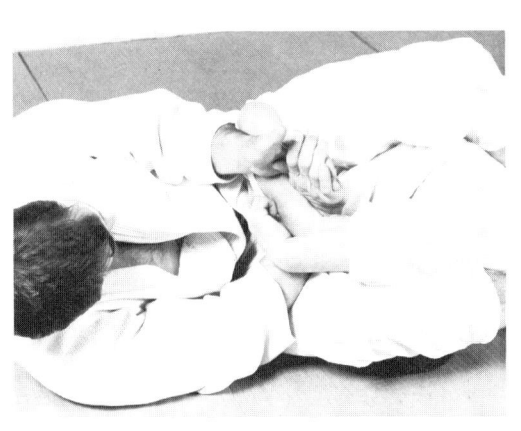

(c) Tori puts his left forearm against uke's left elbow, clasping his own hands together.

(d) To break uke's grip, tori uses his left elbow to block the movement of uke's left arm, pulling uke's right wrist towards himself. He twists the arm while moving his body away from uke's head. The lock is then applied when tori straightens his hips and finishes in the normal way.

FINISHING JUJI-GATAME

Triangle lever *(Fig 29)*

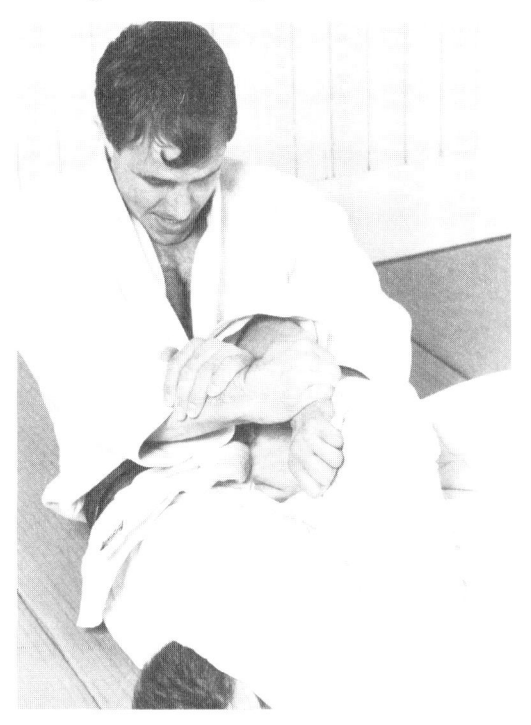

Arm position *(Fig 30)*

Tori grips uke's left wrist with his right hand, passes his left arm under uke's left arm and places his left hand over his own right wrist. Tori pushes uke's wrist downwards and at the same time pulls against the arm, forcing his own wrist into the elbow joint. The arm springs into the extended position saving uke from further discomfort.

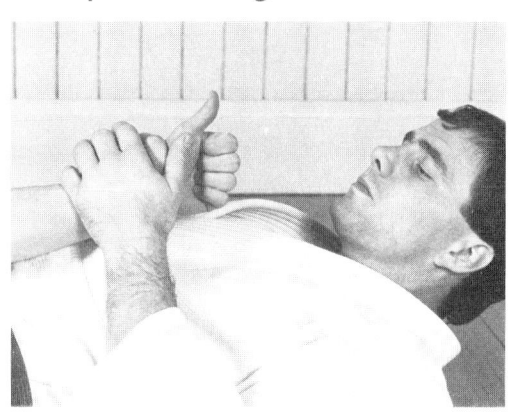

Generally speaking the position of uke's arm in this photograph is the correct position for the application for juji-gatame. A good guideline for tori is to ensure that uke's thumb is pointed upwards when bringing the joint into the locked position. It can sometimes require very careful hip adjustment to lock the arm properly.

Some judoka are extremely supple in the elbow joints and can be difficult to armlock. In the 1982 European Championships against Novotny of Czechoslovakia, I had his arm in a correctly applied armlock position but failed to get a submission because he was double-jointed (his arm must have been made of rubber). Tori therefore needs to practise in a number of variations on this position.

Ude-gatame

Basic ude-gatame *(Fig 31)*
(Arm-hold)

This is Kano's interpretation of *ude-gatame* which appears in the *katame-no-kata*. Tori is in a kneeling position and has locked uke's left arm by pulling the arm against the joint and trapping uke's hand against his own shoulder.

Ushiro-ude-gatame *(Fig 32)*
(Reverse arm-hold)

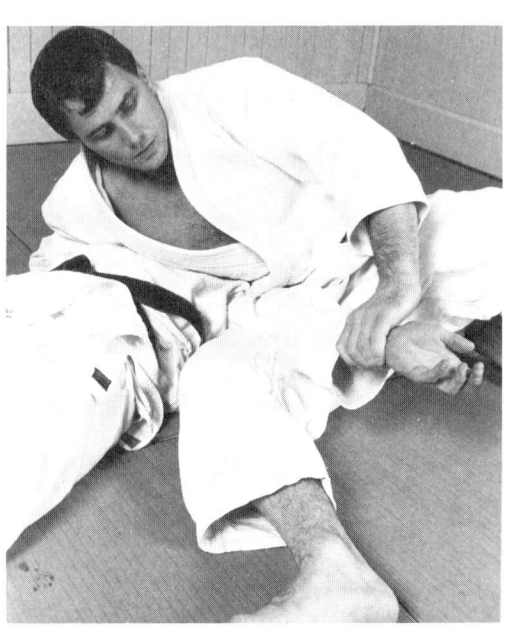

Tori is holding uke in *ushiro-kesa-gatame*. To apply the lock he takes uke's left arm and forces the elbow against the joint across his own right thigh thus forcing uke to submit.

Kesa-gatame with ude-gatame *(Fig 33)*

The application of *hon-kesa-gatame* with ude-gatame is very much the same as in the previous technique. Tori has taken uke's straight right arm and placed it over his right thigh, pushing the arm downwards against the joint.

Reaching ude-gatame *(Fig 34)*
(Off the back)

(a) Tori grips uke's left wrist with his right hand and controls uke with his legs to prevent him escaping.

(b) Tori has now turned on to his right side and passes his left arm over the top of uke's left arm, holding it against the joint.

(c) Lying on his back, tori pushes uke's arm upwards with his right hand.

UDE-GATAME

Ude-gatame *(Fig 35)*
(Basic off the back)

(a) Tori places his right hand across uke's left elbow.

(b) He then turns his hips to the left and simultaneously grips the same elbow with his left hand.

(c) Tori now applies pressure to the joint and forces uke's head into the mat.

Mune-gatame with ude-gatame *(Fig 36)*

Tori is lying across uke's chest and has gripped uke's left wrist with his right hand. Tori then passes his left hand underneath uke's straight arm and places his hand over his own right arm. He now presses downward with his right hand and at the same time with a wrist movement applies pressure upwards against uke's locked elbow joint.

Ushiro-kesa-gatame into mune-gatame with ude-gatame *(Fig 37)*

(a) Tori is holding uke with a conventional ushiro-kesa-gatame and has passed his left hand under uke's left shoulder, trapping uke's left wrist. This is an ideal opportunity for pulling uke's belt over the wrist in order to lock the arm and shoulder.

(b) Preparing as if to pull the belt over uke's arm, tori has forced uke to straighten the arm to prevent this happening.

(c) Tori takes swift action to lock the arm.

Note This combination of three techniques often occurs in competition.

Tate-shiho with ude-gatame *(Fig 38)*

From a conventional *tate-shiho-gatame*, tori has taken uke's right wrist with his right hand, passing his left hand and arm under uke's straight arm and placing his left hand over uke's right forearm.

The important point with this variation is that uke's arm is placed above his own head while the lock is applied, making things awkward for him.

Ude-gatame (Fig 39)

(Newaza wrap-around)

(a) Tori starts the technique in the familiar position on his back, and grips uke's right arm with his left hand.

(b) Tori then turns his hips to the right and simultaneously hooks uke's left arm with his right arm.

(c) Tori then continues to turn his hips, and using his right arm traps uke's left elbow joint, forcing his wrist upwards with his right shoulder.

Ude-garami

Basic ude-garami *(Fig 40)*
(Arm entanglement)

Tori lies across uke's chest and grips his wrist with his left hand. With uke's arm in a bent position, tori passes his right arm underneath it and grips his own left wrist. Tori then applies the lock by arching both his own wrists, lifting uke's elbow upwards with his right arm and forcing uke's wrist downwards.

UDE-GARAMI

Kesa-gatame with ude-garami (Fig 41)

(With the legs)

(a) Tori has applied kesa-gatame and has gripped uke's right wrist with his left hand. Tori now tries to straighten uke's arm by forcing it downwards over his right thigh.

(b) To resist the ude-gatame uke bends his arm upwards towards his own head.

(c) Tori now pushes uke's bent arm downwards towards the mat and traps uke's wrist with his bent right leg. He then applies the lock to uke's arm by pushing his hips forward.

UDE-GARAMI

Ude-garami from ushiro-kesa-gatame *(Fig 42)*

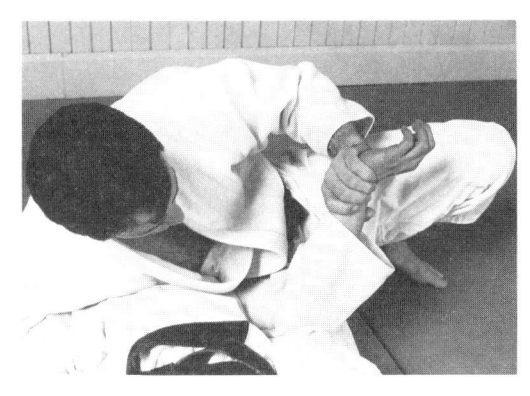

(a) Tori holds uke with ushiro-kesa-gatame and at the same time grips uke's left wrist with his left hand. Tori now tries to force the wrist downwards over his right thigh to lock the arm. Uke bends his arm upwards to prevent the straight armlock.

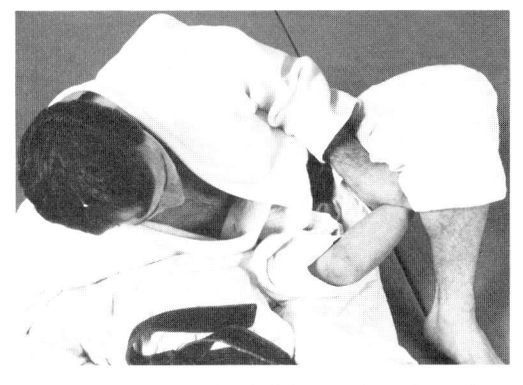

(b) Tori now lifts his left leg and pushes uke's wrist underneath it.

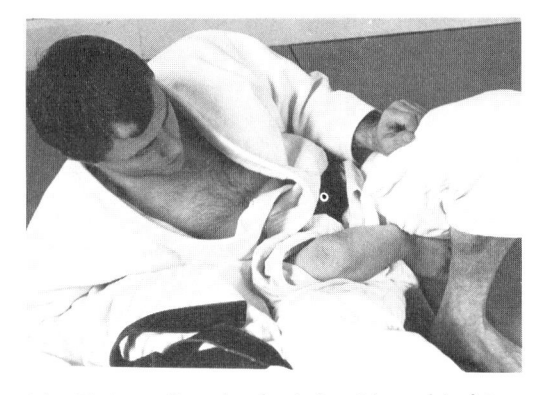

(c) Tori applies the lock by lifting his hips, simultaneously pushing uke's wrist down towards the mat.

Ude-garami *(Fig 43)*

(Off the back)

Tori attacks from off his back and grips uke's left wrist with his right hand. At the same time he takes his left arm around uke's left shoulder and catches his own right wrist with his left hand. Tori applies the armlock by pushing uke's arm upwards towards uke's head.

UDE-GARAMI

Ude-garami *(Fig 44)*

(Off the back, with the legs)

Note In this sequence uke's jacket has been left off so that you can clearly see the control that tori has on uke's left arm throughout the technique.

(a), (b) and (c)   Tori starts the armlock from his back, spinning his body around nearly 180 degrees with the help of uke's belt. Uke's bent left arm is then entangled around tori's right leg.

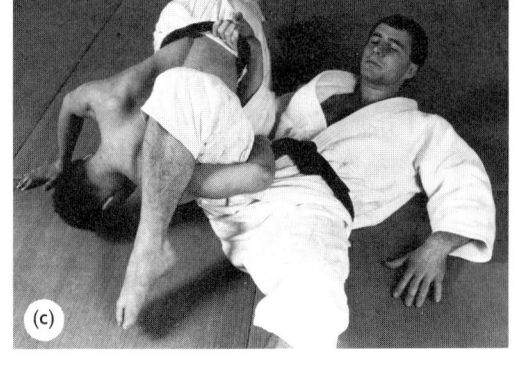

(d)   Tori moves into a sitting position and pushes his hips forwards, bringing his buttocks off the mat. This forces uke's head downwards and pushes his arm up his back.

Ude-garami *(Fig 45)*
(Off the back, into hold)

(a) and (b) Tori attacks uke with *ude-garami* off his back and allows uke to move into a holding position.

(c) Tori uses his to his advantage by maintaining control of uke's left arm and shoulder while he bridges his body, driving uke's body over his head.

(d) Tori now rotates on to his front into a holding position, maintaining control of uke's arm and also his head.

Note This technique should be performed at a reasonable speed as it can be perilous for tori while there is still a possibility of uke holding him down.

Ude-garami *(Fig 46)*

(Off the back, into hold with the legs)

(a), (b), (c) and (d) Tori entangles uke's left arm around tori's right leg, rotating his body so that his head is by uke's left leg. Maintaining control of uke's left arm tori grips uke's left trouser leg and pulls the leg in a circular movement around his head.

(e) He is then in position for a hold-down.

(f) This is the front view of the hold, with tori wrapping his right leg around uke's arm while at the same time gripping the sleeve with his left hand.

(g) The hold-down is then made tighter by tori sitting back on to the arm, trapping it between his calf and thigh. Tori's right arm is used to stabilise the technique.

Sangaku-jime with ude-garami (Fig 47)

(a) Tori applies a 'pillow' *sangaku-jime* to uke, making sure that his right foot is tucked behind his left knee. He then grips uke's right wrist with his right hand, putting him in the correct position to apply the armlock.

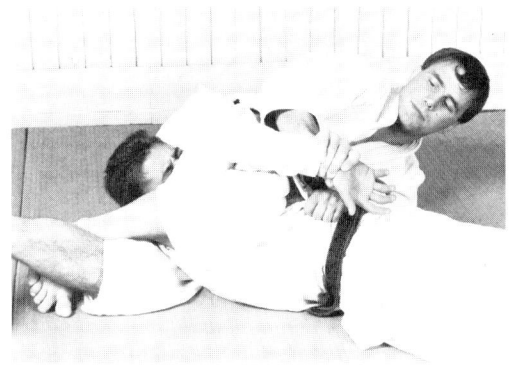

(b) To finish the technique tori pushes uke's arm forwards and at the same time applies the strangle.

UDE-GARAMI

Tate-shiho-gatame with ude-garami *(Fig 48)*

(a) Uke is held down in *hon-tate-shiho-gatame* with tori's right arm around uke's neck. At the same time tori traps uke's right arm across his face with his head.

(b) Tori grips uke's right wrist with his left hand.

(c) He then proceeds to pull the arm in a circle around uke's head.

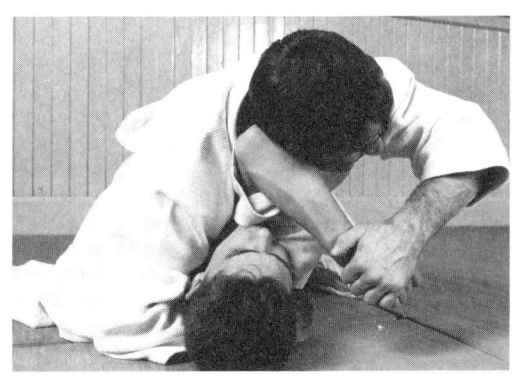

(d) The lock is then applied by tori pushing his head against uke's elbow while at the same time pulling uke's wrist upwards.

Waki-gatame

Waki-gatame is one of the most dangerous armlocks because of the speed, power and total commitment with which it is applied. On many occasions I have seen arms severely damaged after an opponent has applied this technique against the elbow joint. This means that the keynote for training such a movement must be constant control.

Basic waki-gatame *(Fig 49)*

(Armpit hold)

With uke lying face down tori has gripped his left wrist with his left hand. He then pulls his opponent's straight arm upwards and across his chest.

The chest contact on the elbow joint is the key factor for this technique.

WAKI-GATAME

Waki-gatame *(Fig 50)*

(Off the knees)

(a) Uke has attacked tori from the front and has passed his arms around tori's body enabling him to get a firm lapel grip on his opponent. Tori then catches hold of either of uke's elbows and can turn to his left or to his right for the technique.

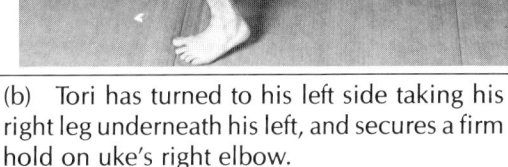

(b) Tori has turned to his left side taking his right leg underneath his left, and secures a firm hold on uke's right elbow.

(c) Tori has rotated his body all the way round and is now facing the same direction as uke. He applies the lock by pulling uke's straight right arm upwards and at the same time across his chest.

58

Standing Armlocks

Ude-gatame *(Fig 51)*
(Tachiwaza wrap-around)

This ude-gatame is another of my favourite armlocks, and I have used this variation since the 1976 All-England championships.

(a) and (b) From a standing position it is easier to obtain the space which is so important to start the movement. Tori does this by moving his right leg backwards, simultaneously wrapping his right arm under and around uke's left arm.

(c) Tori grips uke's elbow joint with both hands and applies pressure against the joint.

(d) To release the pressure of the lock, uke is forced to do a forward roll, and is then in danger of being attacked in newaza.

59

STANDING ARMLOCKS

Waki-gatame

This variation was used against me by Seppo Myllyla of Finland in the final of the 1983 European Championships. It is very effective because while Myllyla maintains control with his right leg, at the same time he commits his whole body-weight against my straight left arm. His right leg is off the ground, preventing me from falling forwards without representing an attempt at a throw.

The lock is then applied in the standing position – at least in theory. In the actual competition I managed to pick up his leg, escape, and go on to throw him for the title.

Fig 52 Myllyla (Finland) attempts to armlock Adams at the 1983 European Men's Final in Paris.

STANDING ARMLOCKS

A short, sharp shock

The following are some examples of the standing armlock used principally to break through an opponent's defensive grip:

1. My opponent is using his left arm like an iron bar to prevent me coming across for my main right hand throws. This is a largely negative action, and I respond to it by applying sharp pressure on the elbow joint. As you can see, both my feet are on the ground – I am not attempting to throw, just to give my opponent a short, sharp shock. If he doesn't relax his arm and change his position, the armlock will take effect in dramatic style. This is what happened in the 1983 British Open when I competed against the left-handed Claussen of Holland.

Fig 53 Adams steps forward as he comes to grips with Claussen of Holland, unsettling him with an attempt at a standing armlock.

STANDING ARMLOCKS

2. Peter Seisenbacher, Austria's double Olympic champion, used a more controversial approach. The rules of judo clearly state that it is illegal to throw with an armlock. Should this series of photographs, taken from the 1986 Europe versus Asia match in Paris, be labelled *ippon* or *hansokumake* ?

Fig 54 shows a technique Seisenbacher used frequently throughout his career.

Fighting left-handed, he grasped his opponent's collar with his left hand and his opponent's right wrist with his right arm. From there he attempted what is best described as a one-handed *uchimata* .

The question remains whether Seisenbacher was deliberately attempting to throw with an armlock or executing a legal manoeuvre which placed him in an ideal armlocking situation.

(a) Note Seisenbacher's left leg off the ground in his uchimata attempt, and the expression of acute pain on his opponent's face.

(b) Seisenbacher clearly pulls his opponent round on the arm.

(c) He takes his opponent down to the ground where he can apply the armlock with the existing grip, or change to a more conventional waki-gatame.

STANDING ARMLOCKS

3. A clear example of my use of ude-gatame in competition to break down the defences of a left-hander – in this case, Gunther Kruger (East Germany), at the 1979 World Championships in Paris.

Fig 55 Neil Adams attempts to armlock Kruger of East Germany.

STANDING ARMLOCKS

4. Another example of a standing armlock attempt – both a genuine attack for a submission and a useful method of unblocking a hard defence. My training partner Ray Stevens is here seen in attack at the 1988 Tournoi de Paris.

Fig 56 Ray Stevens on the offensive at the Tournoi de Paris, 1988.

Hara-gatame

Basic hara-gatame

(Stomach hold)
Stage 1 *(Fig 57)*

(a) Tori commences the technique to the side of uke, gripping uke's collar to control his head.

(b) Tori hooks uke's right arm with his right leg.

(c) To straighten uke's arm and apply the body tori begins to extend his right leg, at the same time pushing his stomach and hips downwards.

Stage 2 *(see Fig 58(b))*
Anticipating the armlock, uke bends his arm around tori's left leg, preventing the first attack. Tori now turns on to his right side taking his left leg upwards and towards uke's head in order to lock the arm. Once again tori exerts downwards pressure with his stomach, and traps uke's head and arm.

Hara-gatame into kata-gatame (Fig 58)

This combination was first seen during the 1985 World Championships in Korea when Ha of Korea caught the very experienced Neureuther of West Germany. A technique will often be all the more effective for being unusual. The important point here is to keep control of uke's arm throughout.

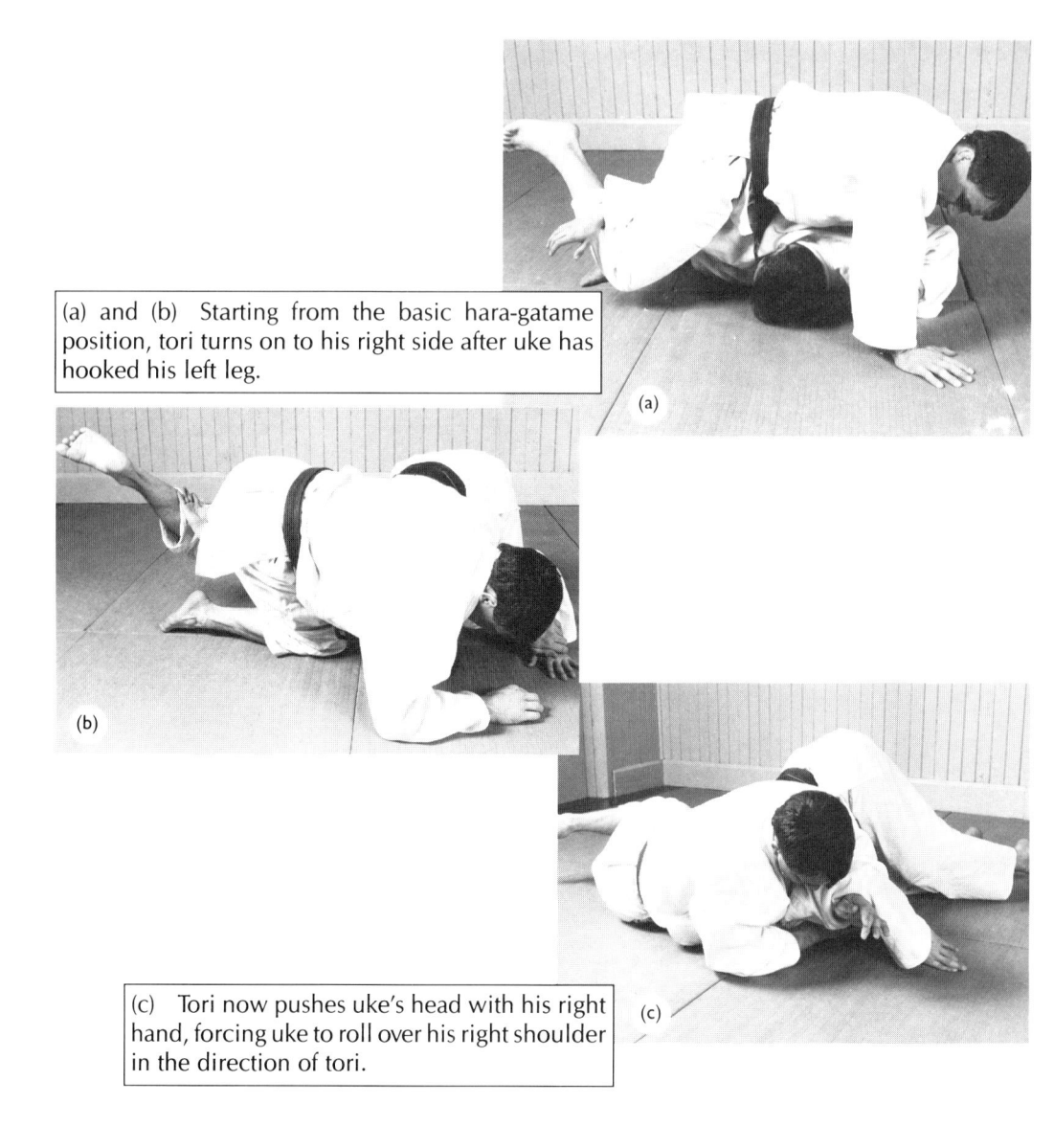

(a) and (b) Starting from the basic hara-gatame position, tori turns on to his right side after uke has hooked his left leg.

(c) Tori now pushes uke's head with his right hand, forcing uke to roll over his right shoulder in the direction of tori.

HARA-GATAME

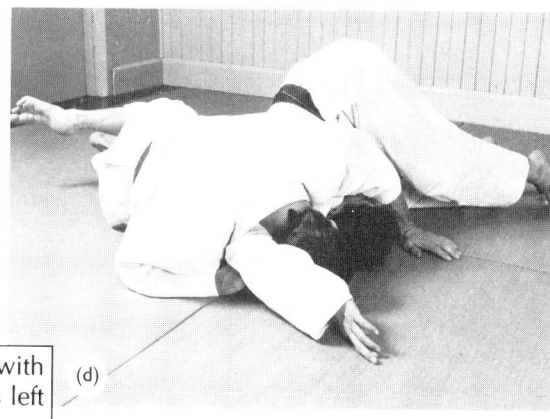

(d) and (e) Tori now traps uke's left arm with his head and at the same time passes his left arm around uke's head.

(f) This is an isolated view of tori's left leg controlling uke's right arm. Throughout the technique tori keeps control of uke's right arm ensuring that the arm is pulled underneath uke's own back once he has been turned over into the hold-down.

Special Combinations

Juji-gatame into hold *(Fig 59)*
(Neil Eckersley)

(a) Tori attacks with juji-gatame in the normal way but finds it difficult to straighten uke's arm. This means that a different attacking position must be adopted.

(b) Tori has now taken his left leg to the right side of uke's head and he uses his right leg to push uke downwards into the mat. It is important that tori has good control of uke's right arm with his left arm so that he can take uke's belt with his right hand, securing a strong hold. Tori's buttocks must be brought up off the mat before the referee will begin the thirty seconds countdown. Tori must be careful that he does not overbalance on to uke's left side. If uke should release his defence of his right arm to try to escape the technique tori must throw his left leg over uke's head and apply the normal juji-gatame.

SPECIAL COMBINATIONS

Fig 60(a) and (b) Both Neil Eckersley and Stephen Gawthorpe perfected the combination move of kesa-gatame into juji-gatame, as Gawthorpe demonstrates here, armlocking in the 1984 European Championships.

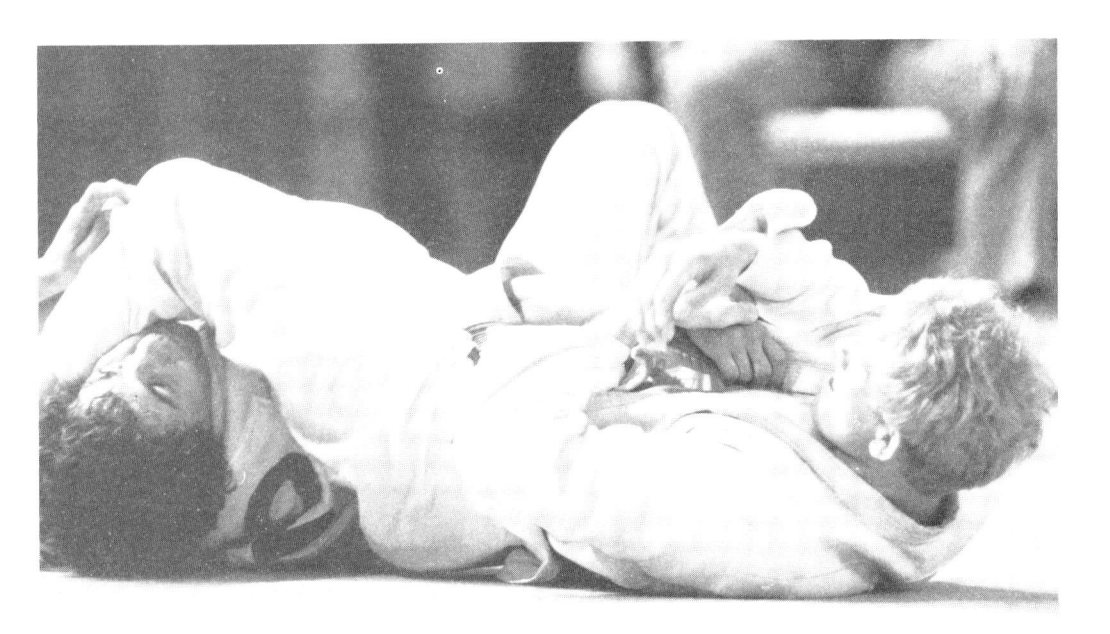

SPECIAL COMBINATIONS

Juji-gatame into tate-shiho-gatame *(Fig 61)*

(Karen Briggs)

Note This variation is quite unusual but Karen Briggs, triple world champion, uses it to great effect and often scores ippons in major competitions.

(a) Tori has moved into the same hold from juji-gatame as in the first combination but this time has taken his left foot further back.

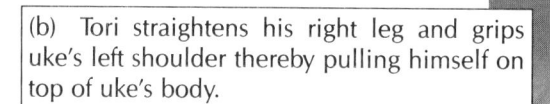

(b) Tori straightens his right leg and grips uke's left shoulder thereby pulling himself on top of uke's body.

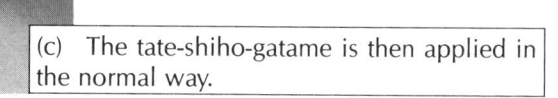

(c) The tate-shiho-gatame is then applied in the normal way.

SPECIAL COMBINATIONS

Juji-gatame into kuzure-kami-shiho-gatame *(Fig 62)*

(With belt tie-up)

(a) Starting from a normal juji-gatame position tori again finds it difficult to pull uke's arm straight and so looks for an alternative.

(b) Tori keeps his left arm hooking uke's left arm and uses his right arm to grip uke's belt. He pulls it upwards towards uke's head and traps the arm with it.

(c) He now takes his left leg to the left side of uke's body and uses uke's trapped arm to help pull himself on top of uke.

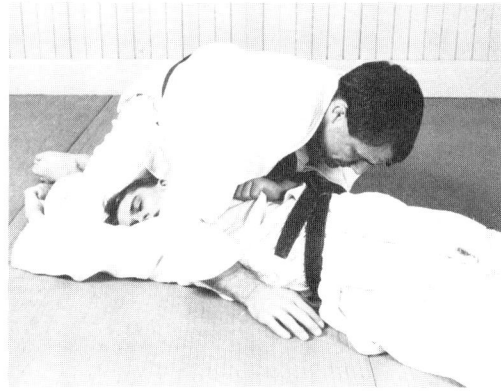

(d) Tori now secures *kuzure-kami-shiho-gatame* ensuring that he keeps control of uke's arm throughout.

SPECIAL COMBINATIONS

Juji-gatame into sangaku-jime

With tori in a normal attacking stance for juji-gatame there are two positions in which he can finish after turning uke on to his back.

Variation 1 *(Fig 63)*

(a) The first position has uke's free arm gripping round tori's leg from below.

(b) Tori leans backwards towards the mat taking his left leg outwards and freeing uke's head. Tori now pulls uke off the ground and passes his right knee around uke's neck.

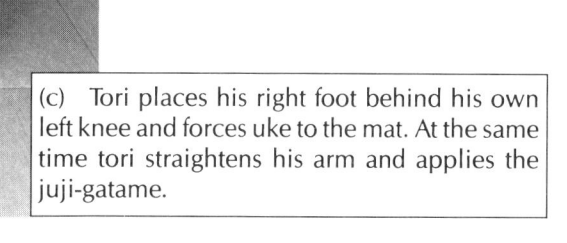

(c) Tori places his right foot behind his own left knee and forces uke to the mat. At the same time tori straightens his arm and applies the juji-gatame.

SPECIAL COMBINATIONS

Variation 2 *(Fig 64)*

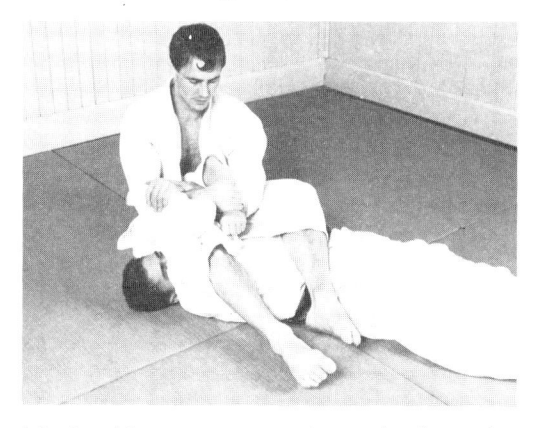

(a) In this sequence tori attacks from the other side, and uke's free arm grips his other sleeve from above.

(b) Tori's legs are facing the same direction as uke's legs, with tori's left foot underneath the left side of uke's body.

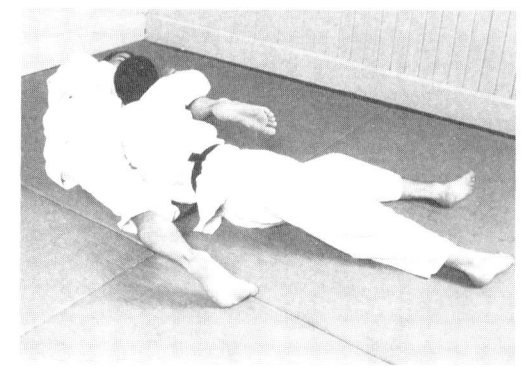

(c) Tori turns on to his left side passing his left leg underneath uke's body.

(d) The technique is completed when tori puts his left thigh under uke's head and wraps his right leg around uke's right arm and shoulder. Tori now puts his right foot behind his left knee and squeezes with his legs to apply the strangle.

SPECIAL COMBINATIONS

Tomoe-nage into juji-gatame
(Fig 65)

(a) Tori commences the combination from a standing position, giving himself enough distance from uke to enable him to begin a *yoko-tomoe-nage* attack.

(b) Keeping control of uke's right sleeve, tori swings his left foot into uke's mid-section and falls towards his own left side in order to throw his opponent with the tomoe-nage.

(c) and (d) To defend against the tomoe-nage uke throws his legs away from tori but leaves his left arm straight and vulnerable.

Tori stretches uke out more by pushing uke's right leg with his left leg.

74

SPECIAL COMBINATIONS

(e) Tori now grips uke's left arm with both hands and turns his own body to his left side, passing his right leg over the top of uke's head. He pushes his hips against the elbow joint and simultaneously pulls the wrist upwards.

Self-defence

The use of joint locks in a self-defence situation can be the most effective way of surprising an attacker, but only if they are well practised. Many books claim to have magic formulas for self-defence, but fail to point out that only practice can give the defender the chance to resist attack.

Waki-gatame *(Fig 66)*

(Straight armlock)

(a) This is a situation often encountered in the street, when the attacker grabs his victim's lapels.

(b) The defender here grips his attacker's left wrist with his left hand, bringing his right arm over the attacker's arm as he extends it by turning.

SELF-DEFENCE

(c) The defender turns his body, keeping control of the attacker's wrist and stepping across the line of his attacker. To apply the lock he pulls the arm across his chest and at the same time continues to rotate his body.

SELF-DEFENCE

Wrist lock *(Fig 67)*

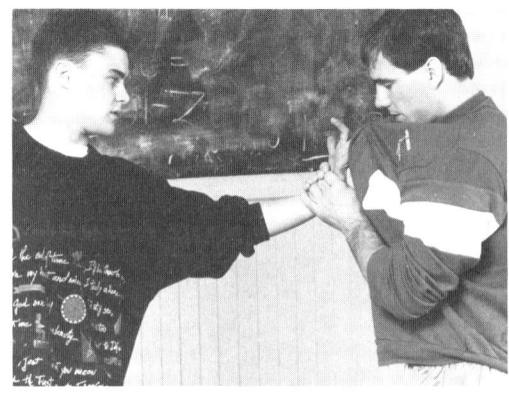

(a) and (b) From the same lapel attack the defender grips the wrist of the attacker with both hands, bending the wrist towards the attacker with thumb pressure on the back of his hand.

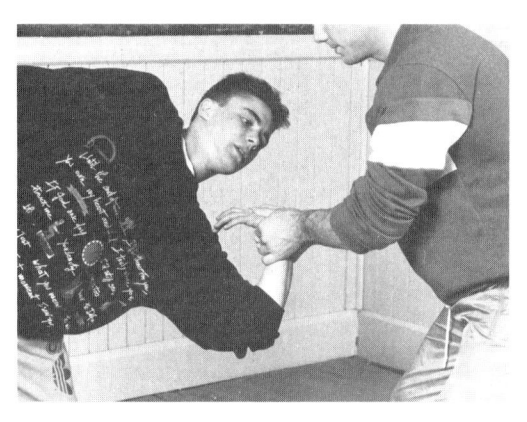

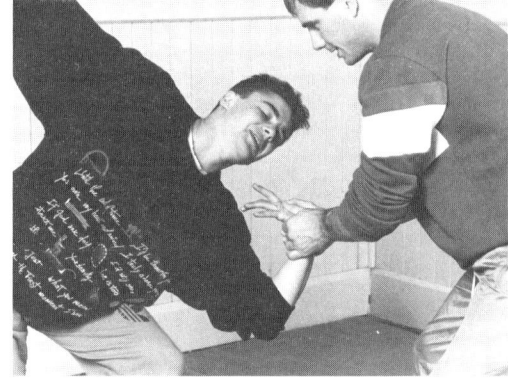

(c) and (d) The defender now forces the wrist in the direction that he would like the attacker to fall and maintains constant pressure on the wrist and hand.

SELF-DEFENCE

Finger locks *(Fig 68)*

One of the best ways of releasing an attacker's grip is by prising the fingers away against their joints.

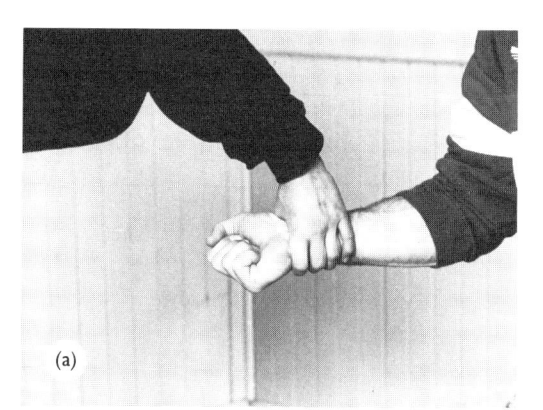

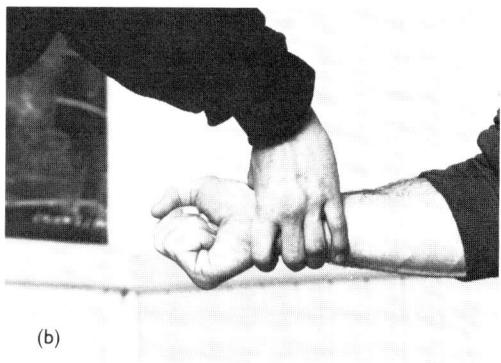

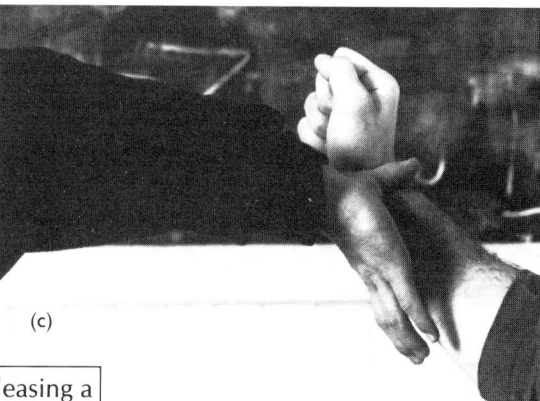

(a)

(b)

(c)

(a), (b) and (c) The simplest method of releasing a wrist grip is by moving the wrist and hand in a circular motion against the attacker's thumb rather than his fingers. This can be done with the attacker gripping the wrist either in the overhand or the underhand position.

Competition Armlocks

The immediate effectiveness of armlocks in general and the clear visibility of techniques such as juji-gatame and waki-gatame in particular, have made them popular among competitors and judo audiences alike.

Even the great Isao Okano, Olympic Champion, World Champion and All-Japan Champion, was not immune. In 1967 he won the All-Japan Championships and was on course for another world title in Salt Lake City. But shortly before the event he took part in a match against a visiting Russian team and was caught in an armlock. At first he refused to submit, but after suffering torn elbow ligaments, and with the contest obviously lost, he tapped his submission. The pressure a champion of his calibre was under could be gauged by the fact that a number of older members of the Kodokan where the event took place felt that Okano should not have submitted but allowed his arm to be broken. However, his injuries were sufficiently serious to prevent him from going to the World Championships in Salt Lake City. His place was taken, incidentally, by Nobuyuki Sato who had fought the same Russian in a second team match in Japan (and, having been advised of the armlock danger, held the man down).

Rarely does a major championship go by without some dramatic event hinging upon an armlock – though this does not always result in a simple or fair victory or defeat. One of the most controversial contests in the 1964 Olympic games centred upon the application of an armlock. Wolfgang Hoffman, the extremely capable West German fighter, had trained in Japan in the years leading up to the Olympics, but had, nevertheless, picked up some of the Soviet armlocking skills. He had demonstrated this in one of the pre-Olympic tournaments. Fighting a leading Japanese, he found his opponent had attacked with a low *tai-otoshi* and, rather ill-advisedly, left his collar-grip hand dangerously extended. Hoffman blocked the tai-otoshi but in the same movement swung a leg over the outstretched arm and crashed down to the ground, applying the armlock as he went. Instant submission followed.

It was that same fierce armlocking aggression that he produced in the Olympics. This time he faced Jimmy Bregman, the United States' great hope for major honours, and a skilled and flexible combatant. During the course of the contest Bregman forged ahead until Hoffman, near the edge of the mat, suddenly attacked with a flying juji-gatame, a technique he had learned from the Soviets. Hoffman had the arm straight, but the pair rolled off the mat and the referee called 'Matte'. However, in the mêlée the armlock was still applied and Bregman tapped his submission in an attempt to prevent serious injury. The referee, seeing the tap, called 'Ippon'. Hoffman was given the fight and went on to win a silver medal while Bregman had to settle for a bronze.

It was not the first controversy surrounding armlocks, nor would it be the last. During the course of the intervening years there has been a whole series of questions raised about the application of waki-gatame in tachiwaza. In the 1970s the East German light middleweight Detlef Ultsch became known for his waki-gatame, which he applied against opponents with a stiff-arm defence. He used to take the opponent down to the ground in the waki-gatame position with such speed that the

COMPETITION ARMLOCKS

victims had difficulty in submitting even if they wanted to, and quite a few of Ultsch's opponents experienced strained tendons and worse. The whole issue of the use of waki-gatame was reviewed, but Chong-Yul Cho (Korea) was still able to use a similar action in the remarkable final of the heavyweight category at the 1985 World Championships in Seoul against Japan's Hitoshi Saito.

Saito had looked pretty well unbeatable throughout the day, and walked forward confidently to take his left collar grip at the start of the final. But in that very first exchange Cho grasped the outstretched arm and exploded into waki-gatame. The two fighters ended up on the ground with Saito flat on his stomach and Cho in the classic waki-gatame position. Saito refused to submit and Cho continued to pull on the massive arm of the Japanese fighter. Eventually, Saito managed to prise his arm free, but after rising to his feet he collapsed in obvious pain. He tried to continue fighting, but found he couldn't grip, and the fight was given to Cho, much to the delight of the home crowd. Saito appealed to the referee, saying it was an illegal move, but the decision was upheld and the result proved to be the upset of the event.

Austria's middleweight Peter Seisenbacher, the only man to win gold medals in two successive Olympiads in judo, used the armlocks effectively throughout his career and he too had his share of controversy. His application of the standing armlock is still talked about even after his retirement, but amidst the many ippons he gained with juji-gatame there have been occasions when his enthusiasm exceeded the rules. One such occasion was in the 1987 European Championships when, fighting Britain's Densign White, he lost the chance of a place in the final by being penalised for continuing to apply an armlock off the mat.

I have lost count of the times I won contests with juji-gatame, but I remember very clearly one contest where it didn't work. I was fighting in the third round of the 1983 European Championships in Liège, Belgium, against an unknown young German. I rolled him three times into the classic juji-gatame position, but each time I was surprised to find that I couldn't straighten the arm. I was well ahead through my standing techniques and so I wasn't too concerned, but it was only the following year that it came to mean a very great deal to me – the German's name on that occasion was Frank Wieneke. Now I know what I should have done in Liège was to switch from juji-gatame to sangaku, but at the time I had total faith in my armlock, having never been stopped before in top competition.

There is no doubt that armlocking is a dangerous business. In the semi-final of the lightweight (under 63 kilos) division of the All-Japan Weight Category Championships in

Fig 69 Saito (Japan) in pain after being armlocked by Cho (Korea) in the over-95 kilos final

1975, Katsuhiko Kashiwazaki faced Yasuhiko Moriwaki. It was a seven-minute contest, and ninety per cent of that time was spent in fierce groundwork. Towards the end, Kashiwazaki caught Moriwaki in an armlock (juji-gatame) and pulled the right arm straight. He heard a snapping sound and although Moriwaki didn't tap, he automatically released the arm. He was very surprised, therefore, to see Moriwaki simply stand up and move back to the starting position with a poker-face to continue the contest even though the arm was evidently disabled. Kashiwazaki took Moriwaki straight back into groundwork and took hold of the left arm. With just thirty seconds of the contest to go he straightened that arm, and this time Moriwaki tapped.

But it doesn't always end that way. In one European championships, Britain's powerful light heavyweight, Dave Starbrook, earned his nickname of 'The Iron Man' when he spent three minutes resisting the armlock attempts of a skilful Russian opponent. The Russian turned Starbrook repeatedly into the juji-gatame position, and on one occasion started to straighten the arm to apply the lock. But Starbrook used his phenomenal strength to pull his arm out of danger. Eventually, the Russian gave up and stood up in despair. Starbrook immediately took hold of him and threw him with tai-otoshi for ippon.

The juji-gatame drama continues up until the present day. Some prime examples from the 1989 Tournoi de Paris epitomise that element of very real danger which is always present when armlocks are used. It is generally advisable, once the arm is straightened, for uke to tap before he or she becomes a victim. In those four days in Paris a number of fighters chose not to, with differing consequences.

Britain's lightweight William Cusack was twice caught in the classic juji-gatame position by Patrick Behague (France) and twice, very skilfully, twisted out by changing the angle as the arm was straightened.

Yoshiyuki Takanami (Japan) was fighting Nahon Gilles (France) in the repêchage of the light-middleweights when he too was caught in juji-gatame. Takanami was a *yuko* ahead from a throw, and decided to brave it out. Gilles straightened the arm, pushed it one way and then another. The audience watched with pained expressions on their faces. Gilles continued to apply pressure and Takanami wriggled one way and then another in an attempt to escape, but refused to submit. Eventually he wriggled out, and the referee called 'Matte'.

Then Takanami took hold again, nursing his torn arm, and tried to continue fighting with one hand, desperate to hold on to his yuko lead. He must have been anguished, however, to see his lead disappear when he was penalised for passivity, and finally was thrown for ippon. Blind courage does not always pay.

Yet Takanami's fellow-countrywoman, Fumiko Esaki, the world bantamweight silver medallist, took much the same gamble when, fighting the Dutch European Champion Jessica Gal, she too was caught in an armlock. Esaki, however, managed to wriggle free and she went on to win the contest with a hold-down to get to the final. Such is the unpredictability of the armlock in contest judo.

There follows a selection of photographs illustrating the use of armlocks in competition:

COMPETITION ARMLOCKS

1 Yastkevich (Soviet Union) armlocking Obadov (Yugoslavia) in the 1980 Olympic games, Moscow *(Fig 70 below)*

83

COMPETITION ARMLOCKS

2 One of my first major successes with rolling juji-gatame was when I armlocked East Germany's European Champion, Gunther Kruger, at the 1979 World Championships in Paris *(Fig 71)*. I had already beaten Kruger in the European Championships in May by throwing him with tai-otoshi, but it was a difficult affair. So I couldn't believe the ease with which, just a few months later, I rolled him from the defensive position into the armlock and then straightened the arm. It gave me a crucial boost in my decision to concentrate on armlocks – a decision which was eventually to lead to my world title. Had the armlock failed, perhaps I would have taken another tack – with a very different result for my judo and my life.

Fig 71

84

COMPETITION ARMLOCKS

3 The start of many a juji-gatame
(Fig 72 below)

For a variety of reasons, none of these armlocks actually resulted in ippon.

(a) Loretta Doyle (Great Britain) at the 1984 World Championships in Vienna.

(b) Thorsten Reissman (East Germany) at the 1980 European Championships, again in Vienna.

(c) Reissman once more, in action at the same tournament.

(d) Adams, also in Vienna in 1980.

COMPETITION ARMLOCKS

4 Even after turning your opponent into the classic juji-gatame position, getting the arm straight can be quite a struggle (*Fig 73, below and opposite*). In the Moscow Olympics, I turned Lehmann of East Germany relatively easily, but as this blow-by-blow sequence shows, I had to use my knowledge of levers to get his arm straight. First of all, I had to control his bridge – he was threatening to somersault out of it. Then I took his arms, which were tightly clasped together, towards his head, and gradually eased them apart for the ippon.

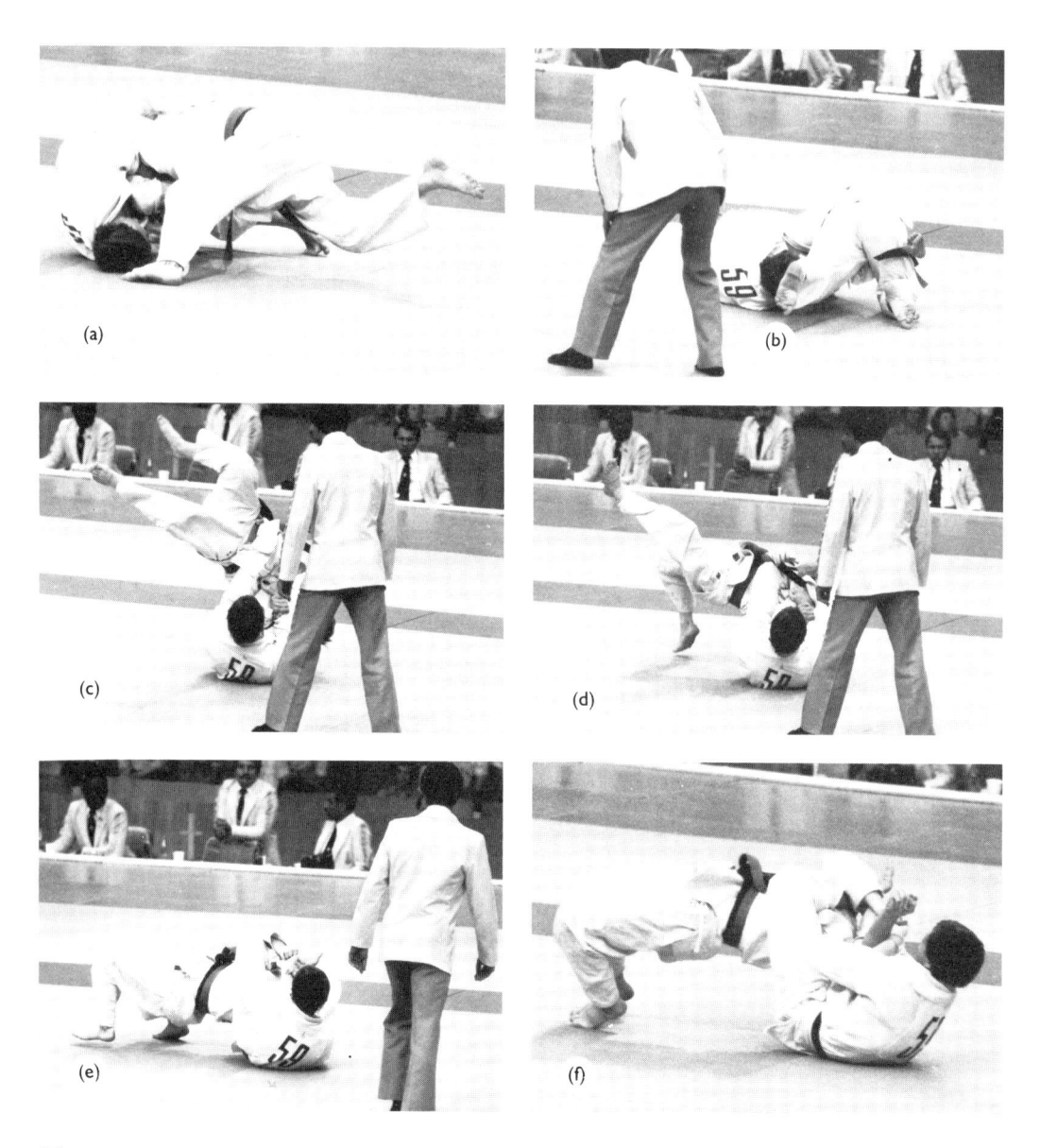

(a)

(b)

(c)

(d)

(e)

(f)

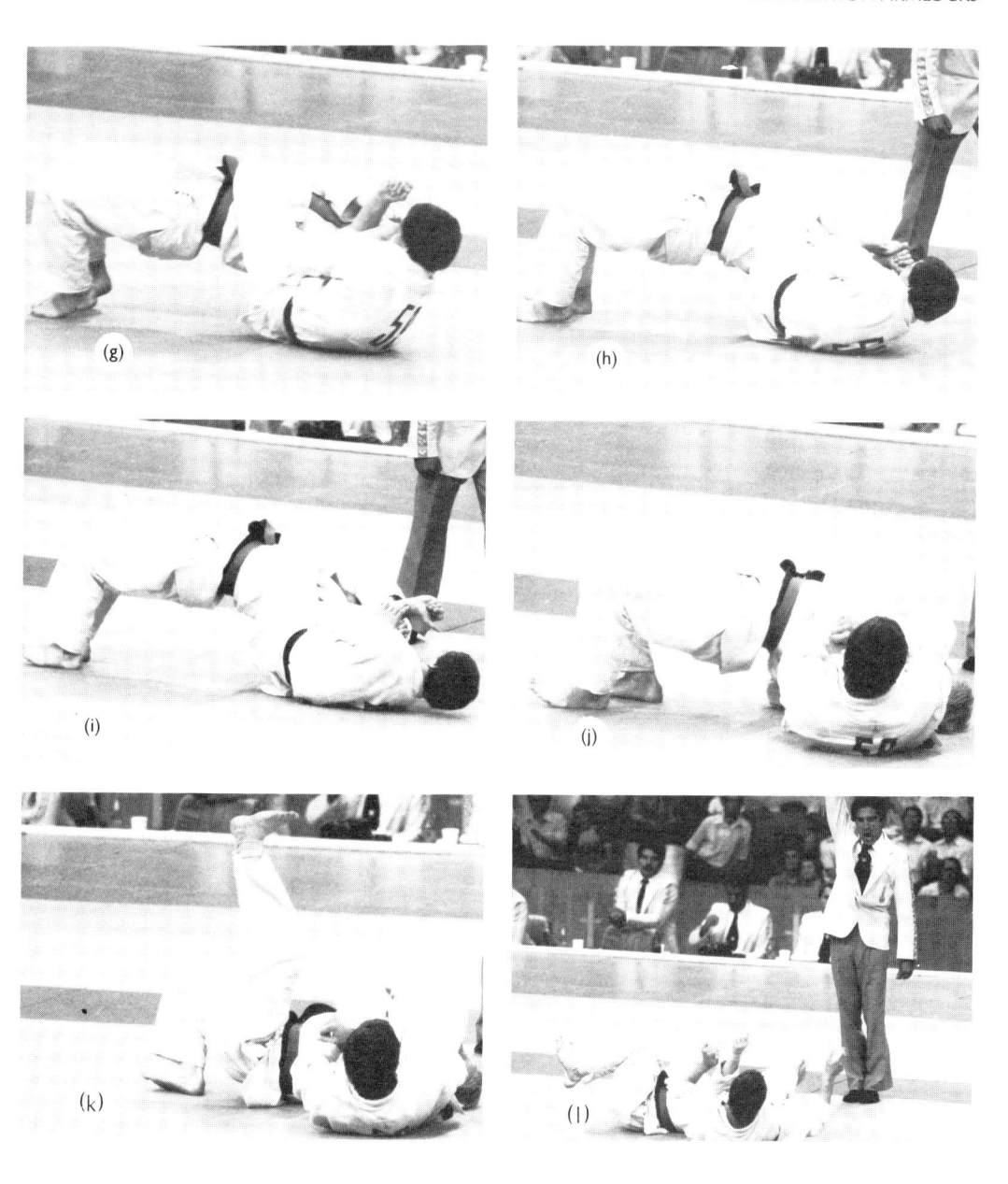

COMPETITION ARMLOCKS

(g)

(h)

(i)

(j)

(k)

(l)

COMPETITION ARMLOCKS

5   In Fig 74 (below) we see how Ezio Gamba (Italy) armlocks Tuma (Czechoslovakia) at the 1982 European Championships in Rostock.

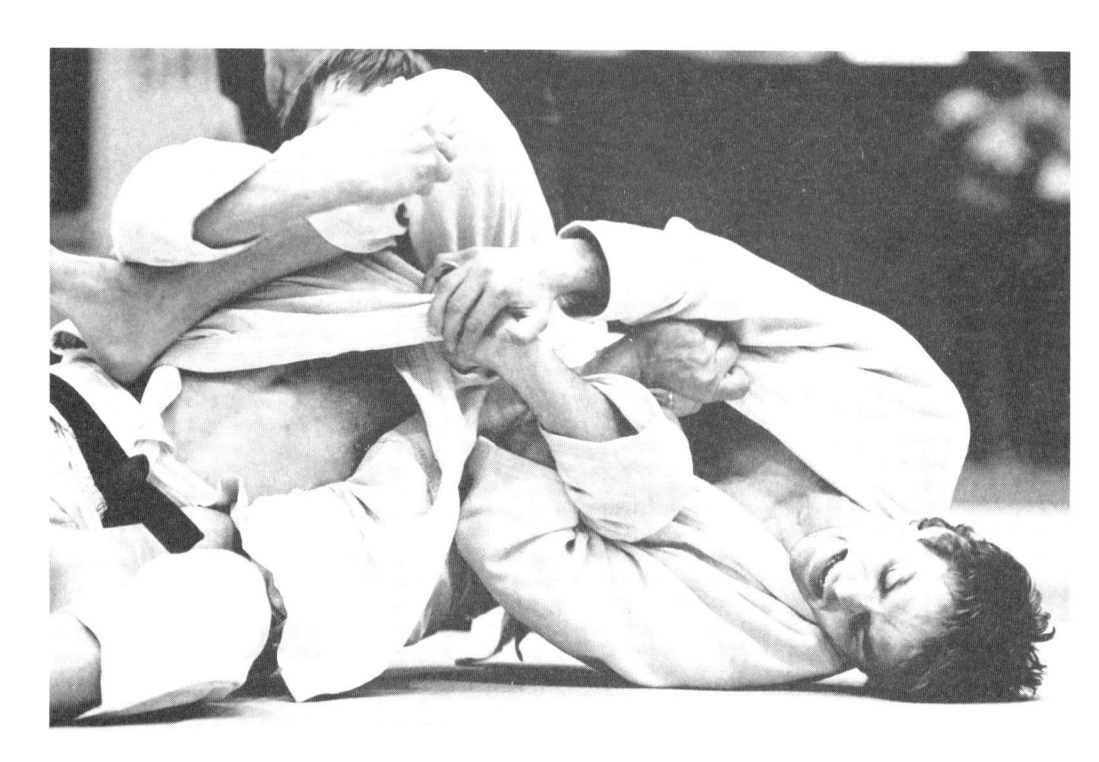

COMPETITION ARMLOCKS

6 Brigitte Deydier, France's triple World Middleweight Champion, armlocks in abandoned style – her opponent is understandably already preparing to tap *(see Fig 75 below)*.

7 Fig 76 (below) shows Ray Stevens (Britain) getting his submission from Kim of Korea in the under 86 kilos category of the Tournoi de Paris 1988 even though he did not turn him into the classic juji-gatame position.

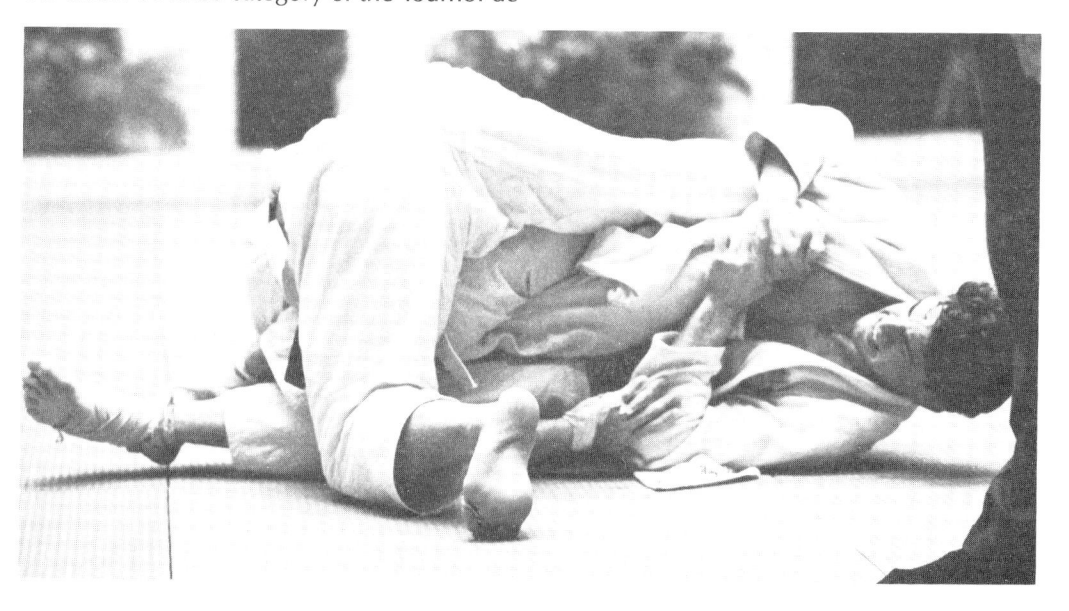

89

COMPETITION ARMLOCKS

8 Fig 77 shows the most satisfying armlock I have ever done – trapping Jiro Kase (Japan) to win the 1981 world light middleweight title in Maastricht, Holland. The contest was punctuated by armlock attempts. I felt very confident that I could win by ippon if I could catch Kase on the ground but he was keen to avoid groundwork.

Half-way through the contest I nearly caught him with an armlock when he was trapped between my legs. He managed to extricate his arm just in time, but was rubbing it as we went back to the middle. I thought I had lost my chance, but a minute later I caught him on the ground again. I jumped on his back and began rolling him into the mat area. We both rolled freely in the best traditions of open judo – he trying every direction he could think of to escape, and I going with him, trying to guide him the way I wanted him to go, never losing control of his left arm and controlling his upper body as well as I could with my legs.

Eventually, he ended up on his back. At first I did not have clean control, as the close-up photograph (a) shows, and he tried to somersault backwards out of it. I pulled him back, and he flattened out so that I was able to cross my legs to exert ideal control and work to straighten the arm as in photograph (b). He twisted and bridged, and I grabbed my own lapel to add extra leverage when I saw his fingers slipping. I pulled a little more, turned up towards the head and the arm came free.

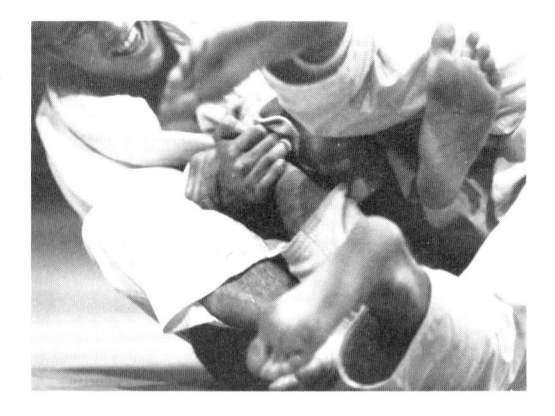

COMPETITION ARMLOCKS

9 In Fig 78 Kris (Czechoslovakia) shows superb control as he throws Ock (Yugoslavia) in the 1983 European Championships in Paris with *osoto-makikomi*, applying a straight armlock as soon as Ock hits the ground. This is another example of a move from a standing position to groundwork that has been practised many times. Kris is not being opportunist here – he has specialised in osoto-makikomi and has almost certainly developed this straight armlock as a natural follow-on. Kris was therefore familiar with this position and as soon as Ock hit the ground, he reached for the armlock rather than for the hold-down. This is the kind of detailed preparation that must be undertaken by all top players.

(a)

(b)

(c)

(d)

COMPETITION ARMLOCKS

10 Fig 79 (below and opposite) shows a perfect example of the importance of practising basics. Judo teachers stress the importance of practising following from standing work straight into groundwork, and the tai-otoshi into juji-gatame move is one of the most common. It is not often seen at the top level of competition because opponents often spin out ready for the groundwork attack. However, this is the opportunity one practises for.

I threw Jacobson (Denmark) with tai-otoshi gaining a *waza-ari*, and went straight into the juji-gatame. Note how I controlled the arm close to my chest, and ended up in the classic position with my right foot tucked under my opponent's side. This exchange took place in the 1981 Men's European Championships in Debrecen, Hungary.

(a)

(b)

(c)

(d)

COMPETITION ARMLOCKS

(e)

Afterword

When competing at the highest international level, a judo player is generally preoccupied with his main contest techniques, and I was no different. Thus it was an enjoyable experience for me, shortly after I retired at the 1988 Olympics, to settle down to write this book and let my mind roam freely over all the armlocks that I had learned, rather than concentrate on just a few.

I was surprised by the fact that more and more variations kept coming to mind, and in the end I had to discipline myself to keep to the main techniques. If I had not done so the book would have reached encyclopaedic proportions, and I suspect that not many readers would have shared my enthusiasm to such an extent!

Over the following months I was gratified to discover, both at training camps and competitions, that the popularity of armlocks among younger players was much in evidence. I am sure that this next generation of judoka will in time introduce their own variations and techniques to add to those included in my book.

I hope that this study of armlocks will serve to inspire competitors and recreational judo players alike, and help to give them as much enjoyment and success from *kansetsu-waza* as I have had.

AFTERWORD

Fig 80 My team-mate Neil Eckersley, 1984 Olympic bantamweight bronze medallist, fighting Eddie Koaz (Israel) in the preliminary rounds. It looks like a hold – but seconds later, in customary style, Eckersley switched to the armlock which gave him instant victory

Fig 81 Martin McSorley of Scotland showing excellent control of his opponent in the middle of his armlock turn in the 1986 British Open

Figs 82 and 83 These two photographs show Yastkevich in action in which he displays the roll that brought him so many wins at international level and that inspired me to concentrate on armlocks

95

Index

Behague, Patric   82
Bregman, Jimmy   80
Briggs, Karen   70

Cho, Chong-Yul   81
Cusack, William   82

Deydier, Brigitte   89
Divisenko, Valery   18, 19
Doyle, Loretta   85

Eckersley, Neil   28, 68, 69
Esaki, Fumiko   82

Gal, Jessica   82
Gamba, Ezio   88
Gawthorpe, Stephen   69
Gilles, Nahon   82

Ha, Houng-Zoo   66
Hoffman, Wolfgang   80

Jacobsen   92

Kano, Jigoro   8, 44
Kase, Jiro   90
Kashiwazaki, Katsuhiko   82
Kris   91
Kruger, Gunther   63, 64

Lehman   86

Moriwaki, Yasuhiko   82
Mylyla, Seppo   60

Neureuther, Gunther   18, 19, 66
Nevzerov, Vladimir   12

Ock   91
Okano, Isao   80

Reissman, Torsten   85

Saito, Hitoshi   81
Sambo   8
Sato, Nobuyuki   80
Seisenbacher, Peter   30, 62, 81
Starbrook, Dave   82
Stevens, Ray   64, 89

Takanami, Yoshiyuki   82

Ultsch, Detlef   80, 81

White, Densign   81
Wieneke, Frank   81

Yastkevich, Vladimir   7, 22, 24, 83